Santa Clara County Free Library

REFERENCE

The Broken Ring:

The Destruction of the California Indians

Great West and Indian Series 46

The Broken Ring:

The Destruction of the California Indians

By VAN H. GARNER, Ph.D.

Westernlore Press . . . 1982 . . . Tucson, Arizona

PRINTED IN UNITED STATES OF AMERICA BY WESTERNLORE PRESS

I want to thank my family and friends who gave me immeasurable help because they believed in the project.

Special thanks goes to my wife and friend, Virginia, and to our tremendously talented friend, Bill Charnley.

TABLE OF CONTENTS

TABLE OF ILLUSTRATIONS

The Broken Ring:

The Destruction of the California Indians

Great West and Indian Series 46

"Ah! my people were strong and powerful then. There were many of them. Uuyot had led them to be a great people. They made a solid ring around the whole earth. Alas! that ring is broken now."

"A Soboba Origin-Myth"
recorded by George Wharton James

An old Pit River Indian named Pintu Hooseh and his bark house.
—Courtesy Smithsonian Institution

Chapter I

THE PIT RIVER INDIANS

On the night of June 4-5, 1970, near the town of Burney in northeastern California, a caravan pulled into Camp Pit, a recreational facility owned by the Pacific Gas and Electric Company and administered by Public Services Employees Association. But unlike hundreds of previous such arrivals, the cars did not disgorge vacationing PG&E employees and their families trying to unwind from a year of eight to five. The occupants of these cars were Pit River Indians, and they were there to claim the camp as their own — not just for two weeks of vacation — but in perpetuity. They explained to the company representatives that the land had never belonged to PG&E and that they would have to leave or be forcefully expelled as trespassers. Following that the Pit Rivers set up camp on the first reclaimed parcel of what was planned to be a revitalized Pit River nation.[1]

The company's response was confusion. Lower echelon officials made various public relations statements to the press about their concern for the plight of Pit River Indians and how they were welcome to temporarily vacation at Camp Pit. Whether these officials were out of touch with higher levels of policy making or were simply lying, the company settled on a different course of action. It demanded that the Indians be removed as trespassers. On Saturday, the 6th, while the new residents were preparing for breakfast, eighty riot-equipped law enforcement officers with police dogs descended on the camp. The Indians calmly explained that they could not be on the land illegally because, in fact, the land was theirs. The beseiging officers answered by clearing the camp and arresting thirty-four on charges of trespass. It should be added that in being arrested the Indians were peaceful and orderly. For their own reasons, not apparent to local officials at the time, the Indians and their supporters were more than willing to be arrested on trespassing charges, so they went peacefully. The charges were presented to Judge Billy C. Covert who released on their own recognizance those Indians who could not post bail. Covert, like many people in the area, knew that the Pit River Indians had a hard life, and if they needed to publicize their plight with this one act, he could let them do it without setting a bail he knew most could not afford.

On Sunday, the 7th, PG&E officials informed the sheriff that the camp was again occupied, and the confrontation then began to turn nasty. Publicity was one thing, but to PG&E and officials at all levels of government, this repeated violation of property rights was something else altogether. On Monday, the 8th, an army of sheriff's deputies, Redding and Anderson Police, State Fish and Game officers, and the Shasta County Sheriff's posse descended on the campground again. Violence by law enforcement was the predominant theme of this confrontation. Many Indians were waiting in the open to be arrested, but others became frightened and took refuge in the cabins located in the camp. Six Indians and four non-Indians were arrested and brought before Judge Covert on Tuesday, the 9th, and among them he recognized some of those released only days before. His spirit of cooperation diminished in light of such defiance, he set bail at $315 in the hope he could prevent more incidents. Such tactics were wasted, however. Even on Tuesday the Indians had occupied Camp Pit for a third time, and this time logs had been felled across

20

access roads to keep police vehicles from reaching the camp. One car managed to get through, however, and seven more were arrested. Judge Covert, openly distressed about the turn of events, disqualified himself as judge on the grounds that he was not familiar with the federal statutes that were being cited in defense of the Indians.

Fifty-one people had been arrested in the three confrontations. Among those arrested was Richard Oaks, the nationally known Indian leader who the previous year had been the first ashore in the occupation of Alcatraz. With Oaks on Alcatraz and also arrested at Camp Pit was Mickey Gemmill, a twenty-six year old student at San Francisco State, and chairman of the Pit River Tribe. Grace Thorp, the daughter of Jim Thorp, had also been arrested. She had given up a lucrative position with a publication firm to dedicate the remainder of her life to the betterment of her people. She dealt with the press.

Even with the public relations expertise of Grace Thorp, it was difficult to convince PG&E or the general public that they were not facing revolution. It was happening at Alcatraz, on the campuses — students had just burned to rubble the Isla Vista branch of the Bank of America — and many were sure it was happening in Pit River country. This fear of revolution was hardly allayed when Richard Oaks announced to the press that the Indians were trying to arrest the president of PG&E for trespassing, but that he was in hiding, and they could not find him. PG&E responded with the kind of clumsiness that comes from angry, powerful corporate executives before the public relations departments can gain control. They closed Camp Pit, accusing the Indians of doing so much damage that it was uninhabitable. It was soon revealed that the police had done virtually all the damage. The company chartered a plane and flew in Ike Leaf, a 64-year-old Pit River Indian who was a staff member of the Intertribal Council of California, and who claimed to be chairman of the Pit Rivers and offered to testify against the fifty-one arrested. It turned out, however, that Leaf had not been chairman since 1965. The press reported his statements for about a month until it became obvious to everyone that he represented himself and PG&E, not the Pit River tribe. Leaf then sank back into ignominious anonymity.

PG&E officials soon learned that clumsy tricks were a waste of time. The Pit River Indians were far too determined to be stopped by accusations that they destroyed a campground or by a threatening old man, even if he was one of their own. On June 11, Aubrey Grossman, representing the Pit River Indians filed a five billion dollar suit against PG&E, Shasta County District Attorney Robert Baker, Sheriff John Balma, and Judge Covert. The suit contended that PG&E was not the legal owner of Camp Pit and that Shasta County officials had violated Indian civil rights by having them arrested for trespassing. The company and the government settled back in the realization that they had been locked into a deliberately contrived case that could prove that non-Indian title to land previously occupied by Pit Rivers was irreversibly flawed. The Indians had deliberately engineered their own arrests on trespass charges so they could draw the battle lines in court. They were ready to claim not only Camp Pit but all the 3.5 million acres of California their people had once occupied.

The Pit Rivers had a strong case. As late as 1856 the Achomawi and Atsugewi, called the Pit Rivers by whites, were undisputed masters of 3.5 million acres in the northeastern corner of the state — roughly the area contained within lines drawn from today's Lassen Volcanic National Park, north to Mount Shasta, then east to Alturas, then south to the present city of Susanville, and west back to Lassen Volcanic Park. In terms of Indian neighbors, the area is north of the Maidu, east of the Yana, south of the Modocs, and west of the Paiutes. When the Treaty of Guadalupe Hidalgo was signed in 1848 transferring California from Mexico to the United States, the only whites who had even seen the Pit River country were a handful of fur trappers and explorers, most of whom came into violent conflict with the Pit Rivers, and none of whom tarried. Even the gold rush failed to shake the Pit River mastery of their land. Tens of thousands of emigrants were foolish enough to use the dangerous Lassen Trail through the heart of Pit River country, but the constant and successful raids on the trains kept emigrants from even resting on the trail, let alone from stopping to settle the land. The few prospectors brave enough to explore the northeast found little to keep them there and hostile Indians to induce them to leave. O. M. Wozencraft, one of the commissioners appointed by President Fillmore in 1850 to negotiate the first California Indian treaties, futilely tried to convince Pit Rivers to join other Indians who had signed treaties. Fearing to venture very far into Pit River territory, he failed to convince the Indians to come out. The Pit River Indians would argue that when the Senate of the United States ratified the Treaty of Guadalupe Hidalgo and the Protocal agreements, it bound the United States government and its citizens to accept such undisputed mastery of the land as title as perfect as any written on paper.[2]

Of course it cannot be a surprise to anyone that whites would not tolerate Pit River supremacy over the land indefinitely. In 1855 a freight road between Yreka and the Sacramento Valley was successfully routed through the Fall River Valley in Pit River country. The road itself was not a threat to Indian dominance of the area. As a matter of fact the road was far from secure. A stage route over the road had to be abandoned after one of its stages was attacked and the driver inflicted with sixteen arrow wounds. The road did, however, bring travelers through the Fall River Valley, rich in timber, water, and arable land. Though this was in the heart of Pit River land, in the winter of 1856-57 a handful of white entrepreneurs decided to winter in the Fall River Valley and thus claim it as their own.

23

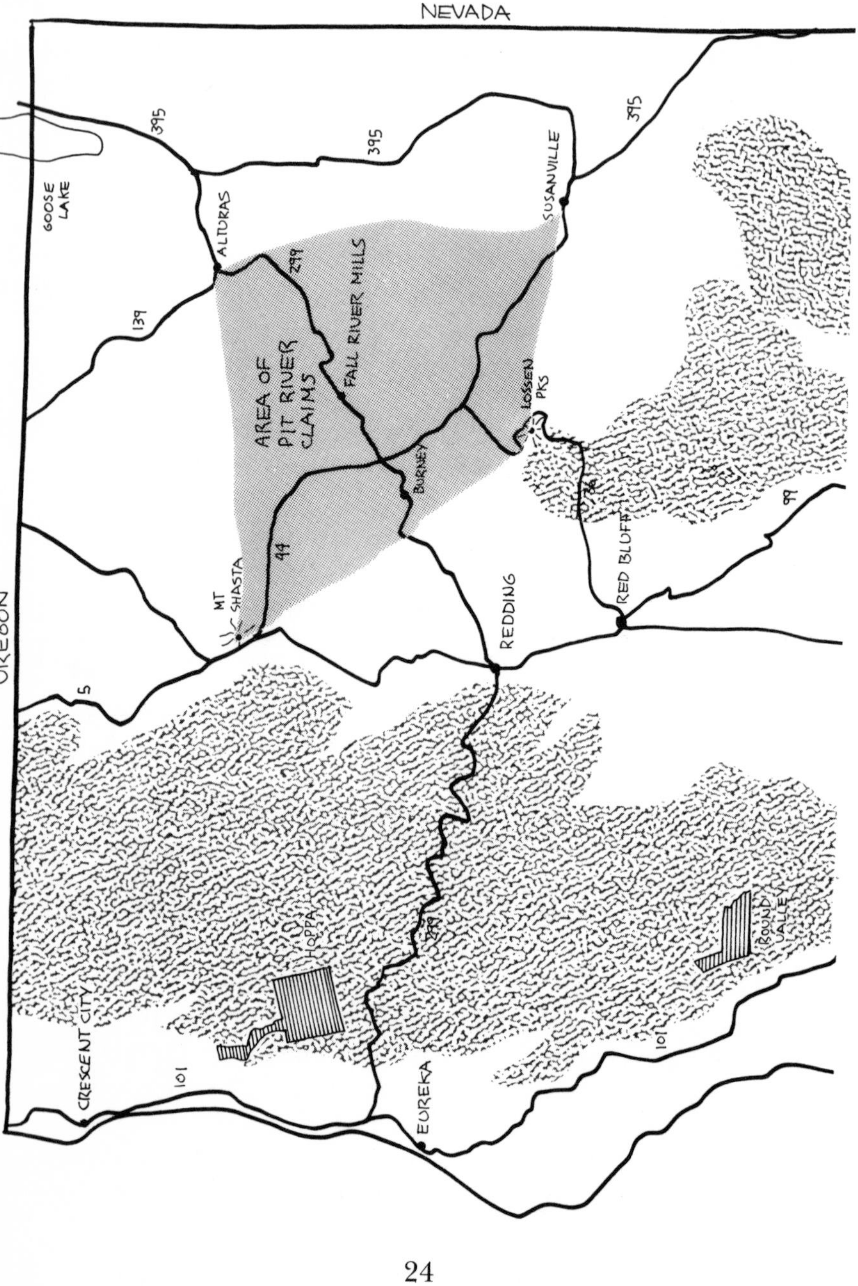

AREA OF
PIT RIVER
CLAIMS

NEVADA

OREGON

GOOSE
LAKE

ALTURAS

SUSANVILLE

MT
SHASTA

FALL RIVER MILLS

LASSEN
PKS

BURNEY

REDDING

RED BLUFF

CRESCENT CITY

EUREKA

ROUND VALLEY

395

395

395

139

299

44

5

299

101

101

99

24

By law, the United States should have stopped such an expropriation of Indian land, but it did not. As a matter of fact, when the Pit Rivers killed the interlopers, the United States financed a series of savage military and paramilitary campaigns against the Indians that not only assured the permanent presence of whites in the area, but assured the nearly complete removal of all Indians as well. In 1857 two federally funded volunteer companies, one recruited in Yreka and the other in Red Bluff, launched vicious campaigns in retaliation for the killing of the white settlers. Between them they killed more than fifty Indians, took a number of women and children captives, and destroyed large stores of Indian food. The regular army also launched a campaign in the same year, killing additional hundreds and destroying countless stores of food. This destruction of food was especially disastrous for the Indians because they were running short even without white military action. The salmon, a major source of nourishment, were no longer surviving the journey from the sea inland because the rivers were so choked with debris unleashed by hydraulic mining. The army was able to prevent attempts to replace stores by building Fort Crook in the Fall River Valley from where soldiers raided the surrounding countryside and thus harassed anyone trying to gather food for the soon approaching winter. With starvation at their door, the surviving Pit River Indians asked for peace and food for the winter. The army officers ceased hostilities and offered some food with authorization of a 1834 law that allowed them to give food to Indians present on ceremonial visits. Army commanders were soon informed, however, that feeding Pit River Indians was in conflict with federal policy. Though individual settlers openly followed a policy of shooting any Indian on sight, the first wave of organized violence was over. By the winter of 1857-58 the less publicized, but no less direct violence of starvation continued to kill the Pit River Indians. The few Indians left in the Fall River Valley survived mostly by working for the few indulgent whites who would give them enough to feed their families.

Even this respite from overt violence was temporary. In mid-August 1859 four whites were killed on Hat Creek, south of the Fall River Valley. Many settlers of the Valley suspected that two of the men had been shot by whites, but they still supported a brother of one of the men killed by forming a volunteer company called the Pit River Rangers whose members planned vengeance on Indians. If any Pit River Indians thought they could share the Fall River Valley with their new white neighbors, the Pit River Rangers ended that idea. For two weeks the rangers did nothing but drink, gamble and eat the free rations supplied by the settlers. Finally they were prodded into taking the field, but rather than go to Hat Creek, they headed for the local farm of Joe Rolfe, who they knew employed Indians to harvest his hay. The rangers surrounded the laborers' camp and prepared to advance. So frenzied was the leader of the group that he announced the attack and then ran in front of the fire of his own men and was killed by a charge of shot in the back. Still the assault continued. Nine Indian men were killed in short order, but the rest escaped. The women and children remained, foolishly thinking that the volunteers would spare them. The volunteers spent a leisure day searching out and dispatching more than forty women and children, many by splitting their skulls with hatchets.

The Pit River Rangers disbanded, but retribution for the four deaths on Hat Creek was not over. The residents of the Fall River Valley had complained to Governor John B. Weller of California that the federal government had not given them adequate protection. As a result, shortly after the slaughter near Rolfe's farm, Willis C. Kibbe, Adjutant General of the State of California, arrived in the Fall River Valley with a detachment of the California State Militia. Kibbe observed that the Indians were totally occupied in gathering and storing food. Army officers told him that the Indians were simply trying to gather enough food to feed themselves during the winter, but Kibbe insisted that they were gathering food for a war against the whites. He launched a campaign against all the Pit River people. The campaign itself resulted in the immediate deaths of only five or six Indians, but Kibbe made sure he destroyed all the Indian's supplies he could find. There was virtally no hope that many Indians could survive the winter, and they began to surrender to Kibbe in the hope of saving themselves and their families from starvation. Kibbe added to these a number of Indians he had captured and transported them southwest to the Round Valley reservation. A few survived in places like Hat Creek, Grasshopper Valley and other locations remote from white settlement, but life was hard. Food was scarce, and Klamath and Modoc Indians raided the Pit River drainage area for Indian slaves whom they sold to whites at the Dalles and Willamet Valley in Oregon. Various attempts were made to convince this handful of remaining Pit River Indians to join the others at Round Valley, but there was little success. The whites at Round Valley did not help matters any when they announced that they would kill any Pit River Indians the government transported to the reservation. By 1869 only a handful of Pit Rivers survived in the Pit River drainage area, and so Fort Crook was abandoned and sold at public auction. Whites were then in undisputed possession of the lands previously held by the Pit Rivers.

If the Pit River Indians had been totally eradicated, the question of Indian title would have been moot, but the Pit Rivers did not cooperate. After being crowded onto Round Valley with other California Indians, the Pit Rivers not only survived, but over the remainder of the nineteenth century some five hundred returned home. Under the humanitarian impulse of the early twentieth century and the Indian New Deal proposed in the Wheeler-Howard Act of 1934, these

27

survivors were able to organize and be recognized as a legitimate tribe of California Indians.

Government attorneys handled the problem created by the Pit River survival with absolute cynicism. As the Pit Rivers argued and as shall be shown in following chapters, the Indians had an unassailable claim to 3.5 million acres of California, so the government's only defense was to use every means to keep the issue of land ownership out of court. Between 1928 and 1944 access to court was actually forbidden by a federal statute called the Jurisdictional Act of 1928. To insure the smooth acceptance of this prohibition, Indians were assigned representation from the Attorney General of California to the exclusion of all others.

Relations between the government and Indians appeared to change in 1944 when the Pit Rivers were freed from the Jurisdictional Act of 1928. Then the Indian Claims Commission was created and legislation was passed allowing Indians to retain attorneys. All this seemed to mark a new day for the Pit River Indians. They joined other California Indians in their mutual suit before the Claims Commission. But when the government thought the case might succeed in winning a huge sum, perhaps billions for the California Indians, the Pit Rivers were forced to separate from the main case. When the attorneys for the overall case agreed to settle for the relatively unsatisfactory sum of 29.1 million dollars, however, the government told the Pit Rivers that they should rejoin the rest of the California Indians and take their share of the settlement, for it was all they could hope to get. The Pit Rivers held a special tribal meeting to vote on the matter, and the offer was soundly rejected, for by this time the Pit Rivers were cognizant of the fact that their claim to 3.5 million acres was unbeatable and was alone worth billions. The Bureau of Indian Affairs acted swiftly to this affrontery to its power by claiming that the Indians acted illegally. Government attorneys argued that the government claimed the sole right to identify the composition

28

of any Indian tribe in the United States and by calling a tribal meeting, the Indians had tried to appropriate the right which these attorneys argued invalidated the vote against the settlement. The Bureau sent out absentee ballots to anyone with as much as 1/128 Pit River heritage. Though the Pit Rivers themselves only recognized a few over 500 members, the government sent out more than 1500 ballots. Even with this devious procedure the vote was close, but this time it was to accept. In 1964 the Bureau declared the Pit Rivers were part of the 29.1 million dollar settlement and that they could appeal the 1964 vote to the Court of Claims, but when they tried, the clerk of the Court of Claims refused to hear them on the grounds that it was not within the Court's jurisdiction to do so. At this juncture it was obvious to the Pit Rivers that if they were to continue in their struggle to regain rights to the land they would have to rethink and reapproach the problem. They needed imagination in their cause, and they were fortunate to find a new attorney, Aubrey Grossman, who began to search for new creative means to get the case to court. This was the purpose of the takeover of Camp Pit in June of 1970 and the 5 billion dollar suit filed in the same month. The action at Camp Pit was just the beginning of a series of similar operations.

On Monday night, June 22, an undetermined number of Pit River Indians under the leadership of Mickey Gemmill drove into Lassen Volcanic National Park and occupied one of the mountain lakes from where they summoned the press and built a huge bonfire to announce their presence. Gemmill publicly announced that the Indians were there to build a village in the park, but he and others privately confided to reporters that their real purpose was to have a certain number of chosen Indians arrested for trespassing, so they could get their land claims into federal court.

By June 22, however, the opposition, federal and county governments as well as PG&E, had already ascertained what the Pit River Indians were up to, and they were no longer willing to cooperate. Indians would still be arrested but on charges other than trespassing. Park Superintendent Richard Boyer approached the Indians and announced that they were all being arrested for starting an illegal campfire. Park rangers, aided by Shasta County Sheriff's deputies then moved in and arrested seventeen men and five women. Others escaped by mingling with campers. All twenty-two were released on their own recognizance.

The Pit Rivers responded by continuing their various occupations, but from this time on with an eye toward better publicizing their case. Raids began on PG&E facilities. On Friday, July 10, newspapers were notified that a raid would take place that night. On Saturday morning PG&E officials reported to the sheriff that their Pit Six powerhouse had been hit. The face of the dam displayed a sign reading "Pit River Indian Nation" and a blue and white flag flew above the dam carrying the same words. On Saturday afternoon the sheriff received word that raiders had felled trees across the various access roads leading to Pit Six powerhouse.

In the meantime the California Judicial Council had chosen Judge William Phelps of Fall River Mills to replace Judge Covert in the case against the 51 arrested in the original occupation of Camp Pit. Judge Phelps did all in his power to destroy any connection between the cases and any assertions about the ultimate ownership of the land involved. On August 13, the *Inter Mountain News* reported that Judge Phelps had said that, "no decision on innocence or guilt in the case would affect the property ownership." Phelps, in the face of all the evidence to the contrary, argued that the Pit Rivers had lost their claim to the land by not filing under a Private Land Claims Act of 1851 and a Survey and Distribution Act of 1853. It is astounding that a judge could make such a ruling on a law that was meant to adjudicate land grant holdings and had absolutely no relevance to the Pit Rivers. The Survey and Distribution Act of 1853 specifically stated, "That this act shall not be construed to authorize any settlement to be made on any tract of land in the occupation or possession of any Indian Tribe, or to grant any preemption right to the same." The fact that no white would venture into Pit River lands in 1853, let alone inform the Indians of such federal laws did not seem to bother Phelps. Exasperating the Indians further, he said that because the Indian Claims Commission had recognized that the Pit River Indians should be compensated for land lost, then the Pit Rivers must not own land, for if they did, no compensation would be due. The government even considered dismissing the charges against the 51 so the issue could be defused entirely. In fact, on September 22, Eugene Chakin, Deputy County Counsel, told the press that he thought Judge Phelps would dismiss charges. On the same day the United States District Court Judge in San Francisco dismissed the 5 billion dollar suit against PG&E officials and the other defendants, giving the Indians a day to file an amended complaint.

The Indians and their attorney responded to the dismissal with vigor. On September 23, Grossman filed the amended suit and this time he added to the list of defendants Governor Ronald Reagan and the State of California on the grounds that the State had participated in the dispossession of the Indians — hardly a flimsy charge considering that Kibbe and the State Militia had evicted most surviving Pit Rivers in 1859. To prevent the government from quietly dropping the trespassing cases, the raids of PG&E installations continued to keep the Indian cause in the public's eye. On September 27, Pit River raiders told two startled whites fishing at PG&E's powerhouse known as Hat Number 2, that they were trespassing on Pit River land. The Indians blocked automobile traffic to the powerhouse by again felling trees across the road. When officers reached the scene the Indians were gone, but the powerhouse was painted with signs claiming the area for the Pit River nation. The same actions were taken at Pit Number 6 powerhouse. In conjunction with these raids the Pit

Rivers demanded that all PG&E dams be removed from the Pit River.

In the meantime, undaunted by the Indian's tactics and the national publicity focused on the Fall River Valley, Judge Phelps continued to prepare for trial. Burney, a town of little more than 4,000 people and center of legal activity, was almost totally involved. Since the judge had decided to try the defendants in five separate trials, and since there would likely be many challenges to remove jurors, 500 prospective jurors, or 100 for each trial, were summoned — a third of the registered voters in the Burney area. Because of the expected crowds, the trial was moved from the courtroom in Burney to the Veterans Building, a quanset hut with much more room.

The push for publicity and more trespassing arrests continued unabated. Led again by Mickey Gemmill, Pit River Indians went to Los Banos in Merced County and picked up a government surplus quanset hut of their own, and on October 4 they erected it at Four Corners near Burney where Highways 89 and 299 intersect, and, unlike in the raids on the powerhouse, this time they stayed. At first the Indians were left alone. The trial for the first defendants began on the 6th, and the government did not want to disrupt the trial with a violent confrontation at Four Corners, and many simply hoped that after a time the Indians would leave. They did not, but on October 10 the jury found the first nine guilty of trespassing. The local paper summarized Grossman's defense as "dramatic, almost brilliant, almost always belligerent." Citing prejudicial local publicity, Grossman appealed for a change of venue for the remaining defendants, but he was denied.

Events at Four Corners, however, would force a change of venue. On the day Judge Phelps sentenced the nine previously convicted Indians to 90 day suspended jail sentences, one year of probation and a fine of $150, the jury selection process commenced again. On October 26, while jurors were still being chosen, the government finally ordered the occupants of Four Corners to evacuate or be arrested. The Indians responded by asking to be peacefully arrested on charges of trespassing, but the government knew the game, and it was no longer willing to play.

At 10:30 on Tuesday morning, the 27th, more than one hundred sheriff's deputies, federal marshals, and forest rangers attacked the Four Corners encampment. Led by Shasta County Sheriff John Balma, United States Marshal Van Court, and Lassen National Forest Supervisor Jim Berlin, the eviction turned into a wild, mace spraying melee which put four Indians in the hospital. Twenty-six Indians were arrested and charged with such offenses as cutting down trees, interfering with officers, assault, and failure to appear in court, but not one was charged with trespassing. Grossman, ignoring a scheduled court appearance, chose to be at Four Corners to protect and advise the Indians being arrested. Clearly irritated by the attorney's absence, Judge Phelps sentenced him to two days in jail and fined him $200 for contempt of court. The judge then agreed to a change of venue on the grounds that the publicity surrounding the arrests would make it difficult for the Indians to receive a fair trial by local citizens.

Moved to Sacramento under Judge Michael Virga and consolidated into one final case, the second trial of the Camp Pit defendants would end much differently than had the first. Delayed for six months by legal maneuvering, the trial began in mid-May and the case Grossman presented was quite simple and compelling. He explained to the jury that the defendants wanted to use the trespass case to bring their land claims to court. If the Indians could establish their claim to the land they could not be convicted of trespassing and, likewise, if they were found innocent, they would thus establish their claim to the land. He related how he told the Indians that if they were arrested, the law followed, they could not be convicted.

On June 10, 1970, final arguments were made in the prosecution and defense of the case. Judge Virga tried to influence the verdict by instructing the jury that he felt that legal title to the land rested with PG&E. On June 13, after three days of deliberation, the jury rejected Judge Virga's opinion and acquitted all 35 of the Indians of trespassing and found only seven guilty of occupying company owned buildings. The seven convictions were not related to the occupation of the land, but only the buildings, and even these were not based on trespass laws but on vagrancy statues designed to allow the break up of student sit-ins. One of the jurors, who worked for the state of California as a land title researcher said after the trial that she felt, "the Indians have a real good court case ... there's a real cloud on that title." She then concluded, "I think PG&E thought it had clear title, but I thought the Indians owned the property."

Grossman anticipated the victory. On July 1, he filed a suit in Superior Court arguing that 30,000 acres of Hearst Corporation held land in Shasta County was Indian land, and it should be returned to its 1852 condition and then returned to the Indians. On June 3, the *Inter Mountain News* of Burney reported that the Indians had sent out letters to eleven corporations stating that the land they occupied would soon be returned to the Indians and demanding that logging operations be halted immediately as they did not want to receive the land in a state of despoilation worse than already existed. Quickly following the victory, on June 16, Grossman filed a trespass suit against PG&E. The suit contended that the Pit River Indians wanted PG&E evicted from all the land occupied by the company in Shasta, Modoc, Lassen, and Siskiyou counties. At the same time the Indians announced that they intended to file similar suits against Southern Pacific, Kimberly Clark, and Times Mirror Corporation. In fact, the Indians continued to file suits until they had included every major corporation holding land in the area.

34

Even as Grossman was filing the suits, he knew that the one acquittal on trespassing charges was not enough to maintain the Pit River claim to their 3.5 million acres. He needed to push the principle into federal court where the real issue of culpability and reparation could be finally settled. In the week beginning on July 18, the Pit Rivers again began to occupy land. This time they took 900 acres of PG&E land near Big Bend, less than 12 miles from Camp Pit. On July 23, members of the press were invited there and the Indians announced that they were going to stay — build cabins, raise children, and plant crops. They even announced that some plowing had already taken place in the hope that a late summer crop could be planted. For the time being the Indians were allowed to stay.

The next targets were the loggers harvesting timber on federal leases. On July 25th trees were felled over logging roads at four locations in Eastern Shasta County and a sign reading "Pit River Indian Land" was nailed to one of the felled trees. In response, the District Ranger of the Forest Service advised the logging firms to resume their harvests, but he ordered no arrests. Beginning in early August, saboteurs struck the logging operations in Pit River Indian country. Damage to equipment was extensive and some operations had to be halted. To allay the fears growing among local residents, Ross Montgomery, speaking for the tribe, told reporters, "We are not out to hurt the little guy. We're not after his land. It's the government and the big corporations who have taken over most of our property. It's them we're interested in. We have no malice or hatred toward anyone—we're just fed up with stepping back." Still there were no arrests.

Neither the federal government nor the large corporations stood by helplessly. Both joined, if not conspiratorially, then coincidentally, in a coordinated legal offensive against the Pit River Indians. Grossman had already seen a preview of this offensive when Judge Phelps ruled that the Pit Rivers had lost their claim to the land by not filing under the 1851 Private Land Claims Act. As unsound as was this position, it continued to be pursued. Ross Montgomery, chairman of the Pit River tribe at the time, and his uncle Gordon Montgomery had been charged with illegally cutting down trees on federal land during the Indian occupation of Four Corners. Neither man denied cutting down trees, but both appealed the illegality of the act on the grounds that the land belonged to the Pit Rivers and not the government, and thus the trees were theirs to cut sown as they pleased. On January 15, 1972, Judge Philip C. Wilkins refused to dismiss the charges, basing his decision on the grounds that the 1851 Private Land Claims Act allowed persons to present claims to the federal government and since the Pit Rivers had not presented those claims before March of 1853 when the act expired and the act of Survey and Distribute Public Land in California was passed, their claims to land were no longer valid. The decision was as ahistorical as had been Judge Phelps', but then the government's case had never been based on historical accuracy. In late February Ross and Gordon Montgomery were convicted of the charges.

Others charged in the Four Corners occupation had better personal fortune than the Montgomerys, but no better luck in establishing the tribe's right to the land. On March 9, 1972, Mickey Gemmill, former Chairman of the Pit River tribe and one of seven tried together, took the stand in his own defense. Although Judge Wilkins had ruled that land ownership was not an issue, Gemmill was allowed to talk about his people and their land. Gemmill appealed to the jury's humanity when he said:

We felt that if we did not get our land back, our people would die off. We were afraid we would become just like the white man. We feel that the world is materialistic, destructive and violent and leads toward death. Indian life is a path to eternal life, and it respects all life . . . Land cannot be sold because we would be selling our heritage . . . this was Mother Earth, and you cannot sell Mother Earth. We cannot sell the bones of our ancestors.

On March 31, the jury reached a verdict. Five Indians were found innocent and a mistrial was declared for the others, and on June 17, the District Attorney dropped the charges against the two. Though these were personal victories, they were of no use in establishing claims to the land — something needed desperately. In mid-November the Indian case for the land suffered a severe setback when the convictions of the original nine Indians found guilty in Burney were upheld. The ruling in effect meant that the court considered that PG&E had sound title to Camp Pit.

The Indians responded to their losses aggressively by staging new demonstrations aimed at forcing arrests on trespassing charges. This time the Indians centered their activities on Forest Service land so they could be assured of getting their case into federal court. On November 27 Indians appeared at logging sites on federal land and told the loggers that they would have to leave. Ignored by the loggers, the next day the Indians tried to halt operations by felling trees across access roads, but success was limited. Demonstrations continued the following day, and truckers were asked not to haul logs from the sites, but they refused to cooperate. Finally Edwards Logging Company was shut down with threats of violence, but on December 5 operations resumed with the protection of sixteen Forest Service agents, six United States Marshals and several Shasta County Sheriff's deputies. The area was ordered closed to all but those involved in logging, and when a number of Pit River Indians violated the closure order, three of them — Ross Montgomery, Talbert Wilson, and Phillip Courts — were arrested.

The government needed to get the timber harvest moving again, and they began an effort to bring an end to these confrontations. James Berlin, Lassen National Forest Supervisor, said the closure order was issued for the Indians' benefit so they could thus be arrested for trespass and then get their case into court. He added in a statement to the press, "We hope this will satisfy Mr. Montgomery and allow timber operations to resume." The government, however, showed no other signs of re-examining the land claims of the Pit River Indians, and on December 15 it announced that checks from the 1963 settlement would be mailed as supposed final payment for land claims. Disruption of logging operations continued. Finally on December 20 a three way telephone conference was arranged among Grossman in San Francisco, Bureau officials in Washington, and the Pit River Indians in the Fall River Valley. In exchange for ceasing the interference with logging the government agreed to re-examine Indian ownership of land by prosecuting Ross Montgomery, Talbert Wilson, and Phillip Courts on trespassing charges for their violation of the closure order. Grossman was also able to obtain from Bureau attorney Richard R. Hite a promise that the Bureau would not use the acceptance of payment to the Indians as grounds for negating future claims.

Soaring Indian spirits plummeted on March 30 when Ross and Gordon Montgomery lost the appeal of their conviction of illegally cutting trees in October of 1970. It was clear that the Montgomery, Wilson, and Courts case would not be enough to establish an Indian claim to the land in the face of such a decision. Indians would have to force the government to file more trespassing charges, and thus on April 3, 1973, at 10 a.m., Ross Montgomery led a small band of Indians in another occupation of Four Corners. The government chose not to respond immediately, but on April 19, a crew of fifteen Forest Service employees moved onto Four Corners with heavy equipment and destroyed the camp. Federal trespassing charges did not follow.

The need for cases to counteract the Ross and Gordon Montgomery precedent was made even more painfully evident as the corporations took quick advantage of the decision against Indian ownership of the land. Their attorneys successfully turned to the 1851 law that had been used against the

Montgomerys and on October 11, 1973, suits against Publishers Forest Products of Burney, Southern Pacific Land Company, Diamond International Company, and PG&E were dismissed by Judge Frank S. Peterson. Fruit Growers Supply Company, the Hearst Corporation, United States Plywood Corporation, and Kimberly Clark soon applied for and received dismissals on the same grounds.

Seriously hurt, the Indians still had the endurance to renew pressure on the government. They entered Shasta Trinity National Forest, cut Christmas trees and set up a Christmas tree stand at Four Corners in full view of anyone who passed by. On November 8, Forestry Service employees impounded 276 white fir trees. Ross Montgomery, George Montgomery, and Pete Wilson were arrested on charges of stealing government property. Without an arrest on trespassing charges other Indians continued to cut Christmas trees until finally in late November, officials from the Department of Agriculture met with Grossman and six members of the Pit River Tribal Council. The officials agreed to recommend to the United States Attorney that the three arrested would be charged under statutes that would allow them to establish a line of defense based on Indian ownership of the land. The Indians in exchange promised to stop cutting trees. As a result of this agreement, formal charges of stealing government property were filed against the three, but either through deviousness or error the statute cited precluded a defense based on Indian ownership of land.

Not surprisingly pressure was reapplied, this time against logging operations. On December 1, Indians began a campaign to shut down logging on Sugarloaf Mountain in the Hat Creek area. On December 13, in absolute control of the area and with logging halted, the Indians hinted that they might agree to move if the government agreed to bring the land claims to court, but the offer was not accepted. On December 14, the loggers tried to return to their work, but were run off by armed Indians. On December 15, forty-five Forest Service law enforcement officers, called in from seven states, occupied Sugarloaf to enforce a closure order prohibiting all but those associated with the logging from entering the area. Thus with armed guards and the closure order, logging resumed. On December 16, the Forest Service arrested Ross Montgomery, George Montgomery, Mary Jane Montgomery, and Arnold Gemmill for entering the area illegally. The United States Attorney, realizing that the Indians could force the government to station armed guards at every logging site in the area, agreed to pursue the real land claims case to court if the Pit Rivers would abandon their tactic of interfering with the loggers. True to his word, before the end of the year, the United States Attorney filed federal trespass charges against the five in United States District Court in Sacramento. Thus between December 1972 and December 1973, the Indians had harassed the government into filing three cases designed to test Indian ownership of land. The middle one was flawed, but the first and the last were sound trespass cases.

If the Indians thought that because the government had agreed to file appropriate charges it would also prosecute in a friendly manner, they were very wrong. All those involved in the cases were convicted in lower court — no one was surprised, but the sentences were harsher than anyone could have expected. Those charged in the 1972 and 1973 violations of closure orders were sentenced to maximum six month sentences with the exception of Arnold Gemmill who was sentenced to an indeterminant term under the Federal Youth Corrections Act. Ross Montgomery, George Montgomery, and Pete Wilson, who were charged with stealing federal property, were sentenced to one year each for Ross and George Montgomery, and Pete Wilson, like Arnold Gemmill, were sentenced to an indeterminant term under the Federal Youth Corrections Act. Grossman combined the cases and appealed.

While the appeals were being processed, Grossman did his best to destroy all future arguments based on misinterpretations of the 1851 California Private Land Claims Act. On March 10, 1975, he appealed the dismissal of Indian suits against the major land holding corporations to the United States Supreme Court. Grossman simply argued historical fact — that no one in 1851 thought that the California Private Land Claims Act affected Indian title to land except in the few cases when Indians were given formal grants to land from the Spanish or Mexican governments. If Indian title was being destroyed in 1851-1853, then what was the purpose of simultaneously negotiating treaties? As Grossman argued:

In Heaven's name what purpose would be served by requiring Indians (assuming that they knew about the act and could comply with it) to file claims for land which they had just divested themselves of by signing a treaty?

He further argued that even if Indians had been required to present their cases, Indians were disqualified from testifying in court under California law. He then asked the court:

Assume, *arguendo,* that this Court concludes Petitioner was required to file under the 1851 Act. We then submit to the Court some hard questions

1. What if the Tribe did not file its claim because its "guardian" fraudulently, or perhaps only negligently, failed to advise it of the passage of the statute and the necessity of filing a claim?
2. What if the Government fraudulently, or perhaps only negligently, failed to advise the Tribe that the treaties had not been ratified, so that claims now had to be filed or else Indian title was lost?
3. What if, because of violence which was financed and assisted by the State or Federal Government, the Tribe was unable to file and prosecute a claim?
4. What if, because of the genocide financed and assisted by the State or Federal Government, the Tribe was unable to file or prosecute its claim because the tribal leadership had been killed or driven off the land?
5. What if the loss of the land meant to the Tribe an almost complete destruction of the Tribe's culture, religion, and economy?
6. What if the loss of the land upon which the Tribe was completely dependent for food and sustenance resulted in the death of a great majority of members of the Tribe since, until 1875, only a white man

41

could obtain public land; and for long after that then only an Indian who had separated himself from his Tribe?

On December 11, the Supreme Court again sidestepped the issue and refused the Indians a hearing.

As good as were Grossman's arguments, they only prove that under certain circumstances, arguments do not make the difference. Grossman made a similar appeal to Judge Hufstedler of the Ninth Circuit Court of Appeals and he received a decision on April 22, 1976. There were some parts of the ruling that superficially seemed to support the position of the Indians. Hufstedler commented about the severe sentences given the defendants, and he reversed the convictions for trespass. He stated that irrefutable evidence proved that the Pit River Indians had occupied the land in question prior to 1850, and in two separate places he mentioned reservations about the government's contention that the 1851 law had eliminated the Pit River Indian claims to that land. Nonetheless, it was evident that this judge was no friend of the Indians. He let the severe sentences of Ross Montgomery, George Montgomery, and Pete Wilson stand, and he dismissed the trespass charges on a technicality, clearly stating that the dismissal would have no meaning for the issue of land ownership. Though he obviosuly felt there was little ground for arguing that the 1851 law ended Pit River claims, he did his best to destroy all future Indian claims with his ruling. Knowing full well that Grossman or another Indian attorney could succeed in undoing the government's interpretation of the 1851 law, Hufstedler turned to another equally unsound argument to block the aspirations of the Pit River Indians. With a total disregard of commitments made in the Treaty of Guadalupe Hidalgo, Hufstedler turned back to Johnson vs. McIntosh of 1823 which had been used as the legal basis for the westward removal of the Creeks, Choctaws, Seminoles, and Cherokees in the 1830's. As will be shown in the following chapter, this decision was the natural outgrowth of imperialis-

42

tic ideas developed during the country's colonial period, but Hufstedler argued for its contemporary applicability when he asserted:

Indian title is a permissive right of occupancy granted by the federal government to the aboriginal possessors of the land. It is 'mere possession not specifically recognized as ownership' and may be extinguished by the federal government at any time.

He added:

Despite 'the policy of the Congress, continued throughout our history, to extinguish Indian title through negotiations rather than by force,' extinguishment need not be accomplished by treaty or voluntary cession. The relevant question is whether the governmental action was intended to be a revocation of Indian occupancy rights, not whether the revocation was effected by permissible means.

This decision by Judge Hufstedler marks the current stage in the Pit River fight for their rights. Though the decision was outrageously ahistorical, it was also uncharacteristically honest. Relying on Johnson vs. McIntosh, Judge Hufstedler had argued, as had Andrew Jackson, that when it comes to Indian rights to the land, the federal government can do whatever it feels like doing, and no one, certainly no Pit River Indians, can do anything about it. Thus with the 1851 California Private Land Claims Act eliminated as a weapon in its legal arsenal, the government is forced to abandon pretense and claim that Indians lost their land because the government wanted to take it. This rationale was enough in 1823 when a majority of Americans thought such an argument made sense. Now, however, the position may be a much more dangerous one to take, but only if today's citizens are different from those who sanctioned the removal of the eastern Indian nations.

A Tolowa man, Old Charley, at the door of a sweat house.
—Courtesy Smithsonian Institution

Chapter II

THE HERITAGE

In 1769, when western man first began to colonize California, he entered a land of some one hundred million acres occupied by three hundred thousand Indians.[1] Today the descendants of those Indians number only forty thousand and hold only a few thousand acres of mostly useless land.[2] When, why, and how this drastic population decline and dispossession occurred is the topic of this book. The reader will soon discover that the pursuit of "when" is essentially a search for those responsible for what happened to the California Indians. "Why" has a relatively simple answer, but "how" leads one through a story so complex that it may never be fully unraveled. Enough can be understood, however, to demonstrate the astonishing fact that the surviving California Indians have a solid claim against the United States government for their rights to three quarters of the state. But we are getting ahead of ourselves.

Five countries have had an interest in California — Russia, Britain, Spain, Mexico, and the United States. All have had their impact on the Indians, even in their demise. More than one had a part in their dispossession, but only one took land as policy and this one is responsible for the bulk of the dispossession noted above. Neither Russia nor Britain is guilty of taking land. They had no interest in dispossessing the Indians. They were interested in furs, not land.

The Russians had little need to deal with California's Indians. Beginning in 1803, in partnership with a Boston merchant and seaman, Joseph O'Cain, the Russians began to harvest the pelts of the numerous sea otters and seals off the California coast. It was O'Cain who convinced the Russians that the greatest profits in California furs were not to be made by trading with the local inhabitants. California Indians were inexperienced sea hunters and simply could not supply the number of pelts needed for the insatiable demands of the trade in the Far East. O'Cain argued that the Russians should recruit Aleutian Indians who were the finest of sea hunters and send them south on hunting expeditions. He reasoned that such skilled hunters working in California's virtually unhunted waters could bring home a fortune to the benefit of all concerned. Indeed, O'Cain went on to prove his point. In October 1803, under contract with the Russians, he sailed south from Russian America with forty Aleutians and twenty of their skin covered boats, called bidarkas, lashed to the deck of his ship. The expedition ranged as far south as Baja California and by June 1804, when O'Cain returned to Arctic waters, his Aleutians had killed and skinned 1,100 animals. With such a successful example, the Russians built a system of floating, nearly self-contained factories for harvesting fur bearing animals. Ships began to carry larger loads of Aleutians, commonly a hundred or more, with over fifty bidarkas. Commonly, an expedition would proceed south from Arctic waters to the California coast and likely spots for successful hunts. The Aleutians disembarked and if the number of otters and seals were limited, they would take what they could and re-embark and all would move on. If an area looked promising for an extended hunt, the ships would go on, leaving behind camps of Aleutians at remote islands or mainland sites. A succession of similar camps might be established down the coast until the mother ship again turned north to regather the hunters and their accumulated furs for the voyage home. Year-round hunting and supply posts were eventually established, most notably Fort Ross near Bodega Bay and a smaller installation on the Farralon Islands off San Francisco, but contacts with Indians were generally limited to small scale exchanges of goods. The character of the Russian presence never changed except that it diminished with the obliteration of otters and seals and with the increased Spanish and Mexican resistance to the Russian intrusions into the south of San Francisco Bay. By 1841 the Russians had virtually lost interest in California. All bases were eventually abandoned, Fort Ross being sold to Captain John Sutter for $30,000.[3]

Great Britain's presence was very much like that of Russia. Her only real interest was in harvesting furs, though in this instance those inland from the coast. She imported large numbers of non-Europeans to help in the harvest — most prominently Iroquois and Sandwich Islanders. It is true that her contacts with indigenous Indians were more frequent because the British were interested in hunting the beaver of the interior, but that contact was almost always peaceful and never dispossessive.

Part of the reason for the limited nature of British activity in California is because the expansion from Canada into the Northwest was under nearly absolute control of the fur traders. In the early years of this expansion two rival companies competed viciously for supremacy, but after 1821, the powerful Hudson's Bay Company gained absolute control of the northwestern fur frontier and solidified itself by building Fort Vancouver on the north bank of the Columbia River. The Hudson's Bay Company set the character of the British presence in Oregon not only because the fur traders set the immediate economic orientation of the British establishment in the northwest, but also because the company resisted all attempts in the coming years to change that orientation. Settlement was the enemy of the fur trade for it tamed the wilderness, interfered with company relations with Indians, and worse yet, lured meddling bureaucrats from urban centers. But in the Northwest, the company had the power to keep the settlers, who inevitably would have taken Indian land, out of its domain.

Hudson's Bay Company employees were interested in harvesting fur bearing animals not in acquiring land. Typically the company would organize a troop of trappers and their families and assign them a stretch of wilderness in which to scour for furs. They took with them their beaver traps, goods for trade with Indians, their weapons, lead, powder, and the pack animals to carry them into the wilderness and the furs back out. Food had to come from the land, from trade with Indians, and from the guns of the hunters who accompanied the expeditions. If these means failed to provide sustenance, and they often did, the horses had to be butchered to keep the expedition going. Certainly the Hudson's Bay Company trappers had more contact with Indians than did the Russians. Being land travelers would assure that, and the Canadians were more successful at hunting beaver than sea otters and seals. This contact, however, was nearly always peaceful because that was company policy — commerce relied on cooperation. Time and time again members of expeditions went out of their way to keep peace with local Indians even though those same Indians had stolen goods and livestock, killed men and animals, and generally made life miserable for the trappers. The trappers did occasionally resort to violence but only under the most threatening circumstances.

Aside from the general British economic orientation that predisposed them to avoid disruptive relations with Indians, let alone dispossess them, most fur trapping took place to the east in what is now Idaho. Interest in California was quite limited. A few parties were sent south in the 1820's and 1830's to explore and trap what beaver they could. None of the returns matched those of the eastern expeditions until late in the 1830's when the yields from Idaho began to drop due to over-trapping. Eventually the company expeditions pioneered a route into California's central valley and seasonal hunting and trapping expeditions were able to denude the area of beaver before the Mexicans or Americans could do the same. Even the great San Francisco Bay was trapped by the brazen Canadians. But these trapping expeditions, unlike those of the Americans, were not forerunners of settlement and dispossession. Unlike the Russians at Fort Ross and the Farralon Islands, the British never established year round bases in California. They would leave that to the Americans who obviously meant to stay.[4]

Though the Russian and British presence was mostly peaceful and not dispossessive in intent, the two countries did leave their marks on the Indians of California, particularly in the north. Both Russians and British destroyed indigenous food sources by ruthlessly harvesting the fur bearing animals. They also introduced goods, especially metal knives, which became important to the Indians, and a certain amount of cultural change followed. And both the Russians and British introduced some diseases exotic to California. There is no doubt, for instance, that Hudson's Bay Company trappers brought malaria to California with devastating results. But none of what they did was dispossessive. The epidemics certainly lowered the population density on some of the land, but the land was not taken as a result. If the Russians and British cannot be held responsible, then what about the Spanish?

The Spanish seem much more likely to have been guilty of the destruction and dispossession of the California Indians. They have a reputation for unmitigated and cruel disregard for Indian life, and unlike the Russians and British, the Spanish had set out to occupy California. Who would be surprised if the Spanish were found responsible for destroying and dispossessing the Indians found in the course of occupation? Certainly most would be surprised to learn that the image of the cruel Spaniard is a myth and that very little dispossession took place. The image of universally vicious Spaniards killing helpless Indians is an outgrowth of wars with other Europeans, not with Indians. The Spanish have fought long hard wars with almost every European nation, and the propaganda and hatred generated by the British and Dutch in particular, have been given unwarranted credence by unquestioning historians who fail to understand the origins of the Spanish image. This "Black Legend" of Spain, as it is sometimes called, has obscured the reality that, over three centuries of occupation in the Americas, the Spanish attained a very symbiotic relationship with the New World's original inhabitants and that such a relationship became institutionalized in Spanish law that ultimately *protected* the Indians of California.[5]

Even before Indians became an integral part of the economy of the Spanish Empire, the government was not inclined to mistreat them. When Columbus returned to Spain with a load of Indian slaves, theologians and Isabella herself were appalled. The Queen ordered a halt to such human exports in the future and demanded that the surviving Indians be returned home as free men. The Church took the stand that all mankind had a right to accept Christianity and become free members of Christendom and Spain's Catholic crown agreed. Thus in 1493, when the Pope granted Spain exclusive dominion over the New World, Isabella was more than willing to promise in exchange that the original inhabitants of the New World would be educated in western ways so they could join the Church as equal members of the Spanish Empire. With the exception of Indians who went to war on Spaniards or practiced cannibalism, the enslavement of Indians was formally prohibited in 1500. Though there would be some early vacillation in enforcing the prohibition, it became a cornerstone of Spanish Indian law.

The Spanish government soon realized there were solid

economic reasons to protect the Indians. Within a few decades after 1492 the Crown found that Spain could not provide the manpower necessary to exploit the resources of the New World. Spain was too sparsely populated to supply emigrants on a large scale, and the Crown refused to accept emigrants of other European countries for fear of introducing Judaism or the heretical Protestantism that was sweeping Europe. Black slaves were used in selected areas and occupations, but their importation on a massive scale was impractical because they were expensive and had a tendency to revolt or escape into the interior. Policy had to center on protecting the lives of the people indigenous to America for they were the only ones who could do the work needed to keep the empire functioning. Officials soon learned that dispossession usually resulted in death by starvation, and because of this the protection of Indian land rights became an integral part of the scheme of things in the Spanish empire. Certainly some Spaniards mistreated, enslaved, and killed many Indians. These abuses were most common during the first fifty years of the empire's existence when the Crown found it impossible to establish much control over its New World domain. The limitations of late 15th and early 16th Century technology made transportation and communication extremely difficult and these limitations made absolute control of a multi-continental empire impossible. Government officials were openly horrified by what was happening to Indians and they actively campaigned to bring the major offenders to justice. And the Crown made every effort to devise a system through which it could control its distant territories and thus protect the Indian inhabitants.

Finally, in 1535, the royal officials thought they had the power and system to establish the Crown's authority and regulate relations between whites and Indians in the empire. In the first application of this system a viceroy (literally, an extension of the King) was sent to New Spain, which centuries later became Mexico, with great discretionary powers in the estab-

An Old Hoopa woman
—Courtesy Smithsonian Institution

52

lishment of sound royal control. The second phase in 1542 brought a second viceroy to the New World, this time to South America, and a new set of laws that strengthened the viceroys and clearly defined the place of the Indians in the empire. The New Laws as they were called abolished Indian slavery forever and formally recognized Indians as citizens of the empire. As the tenth article reads, "Indians are free people and vassals of the Crown, and it has always been the royal purpose to have them treated as such." To illustrate the Crown's problem of control, Peruvian settlers killed the viceroy sent to South America, decapitated him and proudly paraded his head through the highland villages. But in New Spain the viceroy survived.

There are a number of reasons why the viceroy and the New Laws survived in New Spain. Unlike in the south, the viceroy and royal officials diplomatically held off publishing the laws and worked to modify features that bothered the colonists. Simultaneously, the colonists in New Spain were much more amenable to protecting the Indians than had been those in Peru. Most realized that the number of Indians was finite and that the future of the colony was based on their survival as the primary labor force. Various systems of forced labor had always been used, but by 1542, there was a conscious public effort to see that Indians were well treated. There were certain aspects of the law that bothered these northern colonists, but most were willing to see an end to the enslavement of Indians and they were willing to accept Indians as fellow citizens of the empire as long as provisions were made to keep them working. Because of this attitude these principles in the New Laws took root in New Spain. Granted, Indian citizenship was qualified by various systems of forced labor, but as the years progressed, royal laws increasingly mandated that most Indian labor be voluntary and that permissible forced labor be humane. Somewhat paternalistically the crown insisted that Indian ownership of land be communal and centered in villages separate from those of non-Indians. But the isolation was designed to keep avaricious non-Indians off Indian lands, and the corporate organization of a village with land resources gave the Indians the economic and political power base to protect themselves.

Laws refining the protection of Indian rights poured out of Spain. Even unconquered Indians were protected in 1573 with the *Ordenanzas sobre descubrimientos* which forbade armed expeditions into unpacified country. From this time onward missionaries were to be responsible for the pacification of the frontier, while the military would play a secondary supportive role. Admittedly some laws dealing with Indians contradicted previous ones, but all had a common theme. The Indians of the Empire were free citizens and they were to be protected. This principle was the one maintained when Spain's colonial codes were consolidated in the *Recopilacion de leyes de las Indias* of 1681. By 1769, when Spaniards moved into California, they carried with them a tradition of humane missionary expansion into frontier areas and their laws not only guaranteed Indian rights of citizenship, but also protected Indian rights to the land they occupied.

The Spanish continued to protect Indians not only because more than two centuries of tradition conditioned them to do so, but also because such a policy was as applicable to the realities of the Spanish empire in the 18th Century as it had been in the 16th. The Spanish could no more tolerate the extermination of the Indians in California than they could when the New Laws were imposed on New Spain. Though Spaniards claimed California from the time they found it in the 1540's, they made no attempt at occupation. There were not enough people to colonize such a distant land and as long as nations showed no interest in the area there was no reason to colonize it. This was the situation for more than two centuries until the 1760's when other Europeans began to show interest in Spain's northern Pacific territory. Spanish officials

54

thought that if they did not occupy California they might lose it, but there were no more people to spare in 1769 than there had been in the 1540's. The handful of people who could be induced to venture north could hardly justify a claim that California was occupied. There was no dilemma for the Spanish because they could fill California with Spanish citizens by granting such status to the Indians already there. Of course the Indians would have to receive instruction in religion and in conduct expected of a Spaniard, but this could be accomplished by a few missionaries supported by a small number of soldiers and settlers. With the expulsion of the Order of Jesus when its power grew to proportions the Crown could not tolerate, the less political Franciscans were chosen as the most experienced and thus capable of implementing the plan. They had been in New Spain from its beginning and they had proven themselves as frontier colonizers by building mission systems up the eastern part of New Spain into New Mexico, Texas, and Florida. What followed was perhaps the last brilliant undertaking of the Spanish empire.

A small band of Spaniards did indeed establish Spain's claim to California. The Franciscans built an impressive array of twenty-one missions from San Diego to Sonoma, north of San Francisco. Indians were gathered in these self-sufficient missions, sometimes by force, but often quite willingly as a following chapter will illustrate. Since by law it was theoretically impossible to dispossess Indians, the Crown gave the Franciscans only temporary title to the land occupied by the missions. Land was to be returned to the Indians after they learned how to farm it efficiently. Less than two dozen secular grants were given under Spanish rule and these contained clauses excluding any Indian land which might be contained within their boundaries. There was no organized attempt to dispossess or exterminate the Indians of California, for California was an Indian province of the Spanish empire. Dispossession and extermination would have contradicted the entire scheme for the occupation of California. Any attempt by historians to prove the contrary cannot be supported by the evidence.

Historians would have little more success in trying to blame the Mexicans. The Spanish system of accepting Indians as citizens continued after 1821 when California became part of the Mexican nation, for although political ties with Europe were broken by revolution, the economic and legal systems were largely maintained. The Plan of Iguala published on February 24, 1821, and declaring Mexican independence stated:

All the inhabitants of New Spain, without distinction, whether European, Africans or Indians, are citizens of the monarchy, with the rights to be employed in any post according to their merits and virtues.

Mexican liberals, imbued with theories of individualism and the equality of man, pushed Indian citizenship even further. They demanded that old forms of paternalism, which had qualified Indian citizenship under Spain, end so that Indians could take a truly equal place in society. Citizen was the term applied to all Mexicans and when liberals were forced to refer to Indians they resorted to the term "those called Indians" to show that they did not make such racial distinctions. These same liberals dismantled the mission system of California, partly because they opposed corporatism as an impediment to individual competition, and partly because the existence of the missions was an admission that the Indians were a people apart from the rest of the nation. Sufficient land was to be given to Indians so they could live comfortably as citizens of Mexico.[6]

Certainly laws designed to protect and preserve the Indian population were not totally effective. Both Spaniards and Mexicans raided Indian villages to capture slaves and Indians caught stealing food from whites were often executed on the spot. Some Spaniards and Mexicans took land by force or chicanery. This was especially true during the poorly supervised dismantling of the mission system when many Indians did not receive land promised to them. Indians suffered. Between 1769 and 1848 Indian population of California dropped an estimated one third, from 300,000 to 200,000.[7] But the laws protecting Indians were not empty ones. Time and time again they were restated as policy by the Spanish and Mexican governments and enforced whenever possible. And, on the whole, they were obeyed by most whites because it was in their interest to do so. The decrease in population was largely the result of new diseases and it occurred in spite of a desire of the majority to protect the Indians' welfare.[8] There were never more than 4,000 non-Indians residing in California during the years of Spanish or Mexican rule and they needed the Indians as part of the economic system and could not have dispossessed them even if they had wanted to. By 1848, when Mexico finally relinquished sovereignty over California, three quarters of the soon-to-be state was still virtually untouched by non-Indians.

It is surprising that historians would turn to the Spanish and Mexicans in search of those who annihilated and dispossessed the California Indians. A glance at the history of Anglo-American Indian policy shows them to be much more likely candidates. Unlike the Spanish, who developed theories of sovereignty that were based on the successful fulfillment of a papal mandate to convert and assimilate the indigenous New World population, the English claim to American territory was based on the assumption that Indians were inferior and not worth assimilating. The English monarchs of the 16th Century wanted their piece of the New World, but they lacked the organization or resources to colonize it. Their only chance to establish a claim that would be respected by other European monarchs was to assert what came to be known as the doctrine of first discovery — that if an expedition under an English flag discovered land that had not been claimed by another European power, that land became and remained English

MEXICAN CALIFORNIA

even though it might not be immediately occupied. Thus the English argued that they owned the entire area of the future United States because in 1497-1498, John Cabot, sailing under the flag of Henry VII in search of the passage through North America to Cathay, claimed all the land that blocked his way. The problem with this theory, in a legal sense, was that England was asserting sovereignty over land occupied by other people who could likewise assert sovereignty over the land. English political theorists solved the problem by convincing the world and themselves that the Indians of North America were absolutely inferior beings, without government or drive to develop the land they occupied, and that it would be against the laws of God and nature to let them stand in the way of the progress of Europeans.[9]

A number of scholars from the 16th Century to the present have shown that this doctrine of first discovery was nothing more than a preposterous contention argued by England because she had very little else with which she could establish her claim. As Wilcomb E. Washburn states, "the absurdity of gaining possession of a continent by sailing along its coast line was so obvious that some writers facetiously suggested that Europe would have to be conceded to any Indian prince who happened to send a ship to 'discover' it."[10] Likewise the rationalization of Indian inferiority could not be proved with objective fact, for the simple reason that the English made only isolated and sporadic contact with the New World during the entire 16th Century. But no matter how absurd the theory of first discovery might be, it was developed by those who saw it as the key to the overseas growth of a British empire. The arguments based on Indian inferiority came to be believed by the English people, and as English power grew, especially at the end of the 16th Century, she was able to force other European monarchs to accept the doctrine of first discovery as sound international law. The acceptance of this doctrine set the tone of Anglo-American-Indian relations from the time of Jamesown's founding in 1607 to the present day. There was little consideration of incorporating these inferior beings. The Anglo-Americans developed a colonial economy that allowed no place for Indians. Land, acquiring it, and putting it to productive use by individual farmers, was the key to expansion. Indians could not use the land as efficiently as whites and so they had to be removed as did other encumberances on the land. To make the land productive it had to be cleared — cleared of brush, trees, wild animals — and Indians.

In the early years of the United States it appeared that new ideas about the equality of all men might override a colonial heritage that classified Indians as inferior beings. Thomas Jefferson thought that all Indians could be absorbed into the American mainstream. He imagined that all Indians could be induced to give up their nomadic ways and become farmers, as he thought God meant all men to be. As farmers, Indians would need only a fraction of the land previously occupied and thus new land would be opened for white settlers as well. But Jefferson failed to realize that many Indians were already farmers, most notably the Cherokees. More importantly, he failed to realize that most non-farming Indians would not automatically accept the transformation planned for them. And tragically, he failed to understand that whites had an impatient and insatiable greed for land that drove them to any end to get it. The idea of assimilating Indians had some spokesmen until the 1820's, but even during these years, when a tract of land was coveted by whites, it was usually taken with violence if the Indians refused to vacate peacefully.

By the 1820's, the realities of the national compulsion to seize Indian land overrode any pretense of assimilating Indians. Policy returned to the colonial philosophy that rationalized the dispossession of Indians who stood in the way of Anglo-American expansion — in this case an unswerving expansion westward. Americans believed that God had chosen them to spread a new economic productivity across the land. Others, most notably the Indians, could not accomplish the task, not because they were culturally different, but because they were racially deficient. God's command to "Be fruitful and multiply, and replenish the earth, and subdue it," would then also be a command to liberate the land from the Indians as quickly as possible.

If there was ever a question about United States policy toward Indians it ended in 1823 when the United States Supreme Court announced its decision in the case of Johnson and Graham's Lessee vs. William M'Intosh. The case was brought before the court by two men who had acquired land originally given as a grant by the Illinois and Piankeshaw Indians. The plaintiffs argued that their title to the land was sound because it was originally granted by the representatives of independent Indian nations with sovereign rights to the land who could dispose of the land as they saw fit. The Court, through the opinion written by Chief Justice John Marshall, ruled otherwise and in doing so reconfirmed the principle of first discovery. In an obviously pragmatic decision, Marshall argued that the principle of first discovery had been established through the usage of all "civilized" nations and that with the revolution, the United States appropriated all the rights such a principle might bestow. As Marshall wrote:

However extravagant the pretension of converting the discovery of an inhabited country into conquest might appear; if the principle has been asserted in the first instance, and afterwards sustained; if a country has been acquired and held under it; if the property of the great mass of the community originates in it, it becomes the law of the land, and cannot be questioned. So, too, with respect to the concomitant principle, that the Indian inhabitants are to be considered merely as occupants, to be protected, indeed, while in peace, in the possession of their lands, but to be deemed incapable of transfering the absolute title to others. However this restriction may be opposed to natural right, and to the usage of civilized nations, yet, if it be indispensable to that system under which the country has been settled, and be adapted to the actual condition of the two people, it may, perhaps, be supported by reason, and certainly cannot be rejected by courts of justice.

With only scant regard for Marshall's admonition to protect the titleless Indians in peaceful possession of their land, the state and federal governments used this doctrine of first discovery, as expressed by Johnson vs. M'Intosh, as a weapon with which to dispossess eastern Indians. Even as Marshall made his decision, he knew, as did many other Americans, that the British had been wrong in arguing that the Indians were barbarians with no government. Indians, especially in the South and Northeast, were organized into major nations. They lived much as their white neighbors. They slept in cabins, grew crops, tended chickens, and fed their hogs and cattle. As people, the Cherokees had expressed a desire to become citizens of the United States, to become part of the American dream. The only sound justification whites could argue for dispossessing these Indians was a blatant greed for the land they possessed, but this was enough. Using Johnson vs. M'Intosh, such states as Georgia, Alabama, and Mississippi declared through a series of laws that they had inherited the English rights of sovereignty that came with first discovery. They announced that either the Indian nations within state boundaries remove themselves or prepare to be dissolved by the respective state governments.[11] The different nations appealed to Washington, but President Jackson, personally and through members of his administration, told the Indians that he could do nothing for them because Johnson vs. M'Intosh gave the states the rights of sovereignty to Indian lands.[12] He added that if they needed aid in moving west he could help them. Removal was Jackson's goal from the beginning of his term and thus on December 8, 1829, he recommended the passage of a bill that would set aside western territory for Indians who could be convinced to go. Congress complied and on May 28, 1830, Jackson signed the Indian Removal Act.

The Cherokee nation appealed to the United States Supreme Court in an attempt to counter these pressures from state and federal governments. But the Court responded that

Pomo man and woman cracking acorns outside their home.
—Courtesy Smithsonian Institution

it lacked the jurisdiction to enter the case. The Cherokees managed to file a second plea with the Court which was heard and a ruling was issued that forbad Georgia from dismembering the Cherokee nation, but at the same time the Court did nothing when both Jackson and Georgia ignored the ruling. With this kind of cooperation from the federal government, the states pushed hard for removal and one by one the large Southeastern Indian nations succumbed to the relentless pressure. On September 27, 1830, the Choctaws agreed to abandon their lands in Mississippi. On March 24, 1832, Alabama rid itself of the Creeks when they also agreed to move west, and finally on December 29, 1835, the Cherokees agreed as well. The Cherokees procrastinated, but between 1838 and

1839 federal and state troops removed them by force. Of the 17,000 Cherokees who left for their western homes, 4,000 died. The suffering and sorrow was so great that the Cherokees would forever remember the journey west to Oklahoma as the "Trail of Tears."[13]

As long as Spain and Mexico ruled California, its Indians were protected from the rapacious expansion of the United States. But Mexican sovereignty over the land was as vulnerable to Anglo-American greed as that of any people. In a war that lasted from 1846 to 1848, Mexico was forced to accept the "manifest destiny" of the citizens of the United States. With Mexico City occupied by United States troops, Mexican negotiators reluctantly signed the Treaty of Guadalupe Hidalgo that acknowledged the loss of California and most of the Southwest.

Considering traditional relationships between the United States and Indians, it would have been no surprise if the victory had resulted in a treaty of peace that stripped away all legal protection previously given Indians by Spain and Mexico. But this did not happen, for as Mexican negotiators surrendered their territory, they won from the United States the promise that Indians would be accepted as citizens and that land recognized as Indian by Mexico would be so recognized by the United States. This was possible largely because the men negotiating for the United States knew that unless they made the concessions, the Mexican government they were negotiating with would likely fall at the hands of irate Mexican citizens. And they knew that if that happened, the regime would just as likely launch a guerrilla war against the occupying American troops who might be caught in a protracted conflict of indefinite duration.[14] Furthermore, while there was some dissent in the Senate regarding the inclusion of those concessions, the majority, understandably lacking information about the newly acquired territories, had little before them to indicate that there was much land of value in

California except those portions already occupied by whites. And lastly, during the Mexican war, United States policy toward the Indians of California had been conciliatory anyway. Subagents had used gifts and diplomacy in an attempt to keep Indians from raiding white-occupied areas.[15] Under these circumstances there were no apparent reasons not to ratify the treaty even with these protective clauses included. Thus when the Senate ratified the Treaty of Guadalupe Hidalgo on March 10, it committed the United States to continue the Mexican system of white-Indian relations throughout the Southwest.[16]

Though this system for protecting the property rights of the indigenous inhabitants was acceptable to Americans at the time, it quickly proved to be incompatible with the expansion of the United States. No one seriously questioned, or today questions, the fact that on March 10, 1848, by all rules of law, the California Indians were guaranteed exclusive occupation of seventy-five million of California's one hundred million acres. Nonetheless, the situation was destined to change even as the treaty was being ratified. Gold had been discovered in California at Sutter's Mill and emigrants flooded west to get their share. These new Californians, unlike the original hispanic residents, were not content to confine themselves to a limited portion of the territory. They were not willing to recognize any Indian rights. Instead they drove into the interior, plundering, raping, and murdering Indians at will. It was not long before the forty-niners turned to legitimizing this new turn in white-Indian relations by making it an integral part of law in California. This became the task of the constitutional convention of September 1-October 13, 1849, where whites formulated the body of laws under which California would be admitted as a state of the Union.

The representatives at the convention clearly understood the rights guaranteed by the treaty so they set about to neutralize them. The first order of business, as they saw it, was to disenfranchise the Indians. The delegates knew, however, that an outright disenfranchisement would violate the treaty, so they resorted to a thinly disguised ruse which promised Indians the vote at some time in the future when they might be "qualified" as citizens.[17] With the ratification of the constitution by white voters on November 13, 1849, the newly formed legislature set about to continue the task of destroying all the Indian rights that had so recently been guaranteed. On April 23, 1850, the governor signed "An Act for the Government and Protection of Indians." The law had nothing to do with protection. In fact, its provisions put all Indians at the mercy of most whites, no matter how capriciously they might act. Local Justices of the Peace could rule on the ownership of Indian land. No white man could be convicted of an offense through the testimony of an Indian. An Indian convicted of stealing horses, mules, cattle or any valuable object was subject to the lash. Able bodied Indians caught loitering could be arrested on the complaint of any white citizen. Any local Justice of the Peace, Mayor or Recorder could convict the Indian and subsequently hire him or her out, within twenty-four hours, to the highest bidder. As a matter of fact, any Indian convicted of a crime for which there was a fine he could not pay could be hired in just the same way. Finally, the bill legalized the enslavement of young Indians under a vaguely worded indenturement provision that allowed whites to claim the labor of Indian minors. The claimants only had to state that the children were not taken under compulsion. But of course, no Indians could dispute such a claim in court because such testimony was not accepted. Indians had thus been disenfranchised and whites were allowed to take Indian land almost at will. Indians had virtually no rights in court and whites could even claim their labor under a number of conveniently established pretenses.

When California applied for statehood, there was no doubt in Washington what acceptance would mean for the

Indians. The California constitution and the "Act for the Government and Protection of Indians" were part of the public record. Besides this, the federal government had sent investigators to California on fact-finding expeditions and they had confirmed the traditional rights of Indians and their extensive land claims based on these rights. In unison, the investigators told of the nearly total disregard for these rights and the tremendous suffering which resulted from this disregard.[18]

Because of the obligation incurred in the Treaty of Guadalupe Hidalgo, the United States should have rejected California's bid for statehood and sent in troops to restore order, but this the government was not willing to do. First, the admission of California, no matter what her constitution, was an integral part of the Compromise of 1850. The Union itself was at stake and no rights of Indians would stand in the way of a mechanism for holding it together. Even if Congress had decided to protect California Indians it would have had to appropriate huge sums for the support of troops and this would have been in the face of violent public opposition. Most Anglo-Americans of the time, and the press that spoke for them, saw the conquest of *all* California as inevitable and part of the manifest destiny of the United States, and this conquest could only be accomplished if the Indians were removed. The Indians of California would have to give way, and federal policy would have to diverge from the promises made in the treaty with Mexico. So with a clear understanding of their responsibilities under the treaty, Washington officials turned their backs on the rights of the California Indians.

Even with the admission of California as a state on September 9, 1850, the federal government began to give away Indian land. 500,000 acres were given the state under a federal law of September 4, 1841, which granted land to all states so they could generate funds for internal improvement. Nineteen days later, on September 28, another federal law granted California all the swamp and overflow lands within its bor-

AREAS THAT WERE TO BE
CEDED BY THE UNRATIFIED
TREATIES WITH
CALIFORNIA TRIBES
IN 1851 AND 1852

ders. Because California could define such lands and since, in Horace Greely's words, much of the land eventually selected, "had not enough muck on the surface to accommodate a single fair sized frog," California thus gained several million good acres—most of it belonging to Indians.[19]

This initial "donation" was nothing compared to what would soon follow. Federal authorities turned their attention to destroying Indian title to the bulk of the 75 million acres they still possessed. The plan was to force the Indians to vacate the land they possessed. Part of this was a continuation of the policy of removal used to displace the Indians in the eastern United States, but most of it was something else altogether. The inspectors sent to California had indicated that Mexican law had recognized Indian occupation as proof of title to land, but the reports also stated that this title was not necessarily permanent. If the land should be abandoned at any time, it became open for occupation by others. Anyone familiar with California knew that the Indians were experiencing depredations of every description, and no end in sight, they might accept offers of protection on reservations, no matter how limited the acreage. To accept such an offer, the Indians would have to abandon possession and consequently title to large tracts of land they had historically occupied. In October 1850, President Fillmore put such a plan into effect when he appointed California Commissioners to sign treaties with the California Indians through which they would agree to move to reservations.[20]

The plan worked better than the most avaricious whites might have hoped. In violence-filled California the inequity of having to exchange their lives for their land was not of immediate importance to the Indians. A total of 18 treaties were negotiated and signed by chiefs and headmen representing approximately half the Indians of California. Though treaties were not signed with all California Indians, most were effected since the establishment of reservations gave whites the excuse to forceably drive thousands of neighboring Indians to the nearest one. Indian lands were thus pared down to a mere 8.5 million acres, only slightly more than a tenth of what they had been.[21]

It must be added that there is every indication that the Commissioners negotiating these treaties did so with the honest intention of providing the Indians with some sort of decent future. For instance, in the Treaty of Temecula negotiated in the southern part of the state, the Commissioners promised that the government would hire teachers who would help the Indians learn trades useful in the white world. They promised 2,500 head of healthy cattle, 350 hundred pound sacks of flour, a variety of agricultural implements and clothes. With assurances that the Senate of the United States would automatically ratify the 18 treaties, tens of thousands of California Indians began the trek to their new lands.[22]

Unfortunately the promises made by the Commissioners proved again that the road to hell is paved with good intentions. Events in California were leading to a situation that neither the negotiators nor the Indians had anticipated. The California legislature was in violent opposition to any plan which might guarantee Indians the possession of even those 8.5 million acres promised in the federal treaties. In fact, among the serious considerations in those early sessions after statehood was a plan for the total evacuation of California's Indians to Indian territory in Oklahoma. So it should be no surprise that the California Legislature ordered its first federal senators to do all in their power to stop the ratification of the 18 treaties. They in turn argued to their colleagues in Washington that the 8.5 million acres of land set aside for reservations were worth at least 100 million dollars and that it would be a waste to give Indians property of this value. Other senators scrambled to please the newly arrived Californians whose votes held the balance of power in a vicious struggle between Whigs and Democrats. Predictably, on July 8, 1852, the Indian treaties were flatly rejected.[23]

Thus in one stroke the Senate had dispossessed most California Indians of their land. Homes vacated under the provisions of the 18 treaties, the prodding of the Commissioners, or the threats of local settlers, were soon reoccupied by whites and when the Indians arrived at the assigned reservations, they were run off by other whites who successfully claimed even this land as their own. It is ironic that this failure to ratify the treaties prevented the majority of the California Indians from *voluntarily* giving up their legal claim to huge amounts of land for they could still claim 75 million acres that had been occupied under the rule of Spain and Mexico and was guaranteed to them by the treaty of Guadalupe Hidalgo. Nevertheless, the fact was that the Indians were no longer in possession of the land and had thus, in all practical terms, lost it. Staggering legal questions remained, but reconciling them with the real situation was postponed because the treaties were classified secret and buried in the archives for half a century.

Even while the treaties were being negotiated, the federal government was working to dispossess another group of Indians who were not as easily bullied because they held paper title to the land they occupied. Mostly the remnants of mission populations, these Indians had either been given grants themselves or were living on white held grants which had been conferred with the stipulation that the rights of Indians within their boundaries be guaranteed. On March 3, 1851, a federal law was passed "to ascertain the private land claims in the state of California." Under this law the President appointed a commission with the power to substantiate or invalidate land grants issued by the Spanish and Mexican governments. All individuals or groups claiming title under Spanish or Mexican law were supposed to present a case for title before the commission within two years or lose the land which would then become part of the public domain. Parenthetically, the government did not include in this process the vast majority of Indians who held title by custom rather than grant because they were already agreeing to abandon their lands under the 18 treaties, and no one wanted them to claim title to land under the March 3 law when they were already agreeing to give up that same land. There is no indication that any of them were told of the commission's existence. Even if they had been told they would have seen no reason to appear, for they would have had every reason to believe that the government was giving them title to land, albeit limited in extent under one of the 18 treaties.

As might be expected, few of the grant holding Indians were informed of the commission's existence either, and since they had to know before they could present their cases, this was the same as terminating their grants. Out of 40 grants made to Indians, only 22 were presented before the commission. Of these, 13 were presented by whites who had already come into possession of the land. Out of the remaining nine claims, only six were confirmed.[24] Most Indian grants which were not confirmed became part of the public domain under procedures established in a March 3, 1853, law entitled "An act to provide for the survey of public lands in California, the granting of preemption rights therein, and for other purposes." The commission also invalidated 232 out of 813 claims presented by whites, and that land, including Indian occupied land within the grants also became part of the public domain.[25] The only Indians left unmolested were those whose homes were contained within grants whose white owners managed to have them confirmed. But the commission set the stage for their dispossession as well, for when it validated these grants, it failed to document the areas within them occupied by Indians. Without such documentation, white owners found it quite easy to evict unwanted residents.[26]

There is only one bright side to this process of ascertaining the private land claims in California, and that is section 6 of the 1853 law which reads, "That this act shall not be construed to authorize any settlement to be made on any tract of land in occupation or possession of any tribe, or to grant any preemption right to the same." Thus, much to the chagrin of 20th Century government attorneys, the law had inadvertently confirmed on paper that the March 3 laws did not apply to all Indians because they left some Indian title intact. In 1856 the California legislature confirmed the continuation of sound Indian title when it passed a joint resolution, "That our Senators and Representatives in Congress be requested to urge upon Congress the necessity of immediate action to provide some means for the extinguishment of 'Indian Titles,' to lands in this State."

Despite the fact that the process of treaty making and the two March 3 laws were not as thorough in destroying title as some might have liked, they were extremely effective in physically dispossessing most of the California Indians. Thus of all the nations which had been active in California, the United States was the first one to intentionally assume the role of dispossessor. This stance never changed. It only became less honest as it became part of the incredibly destructive California reservation system.

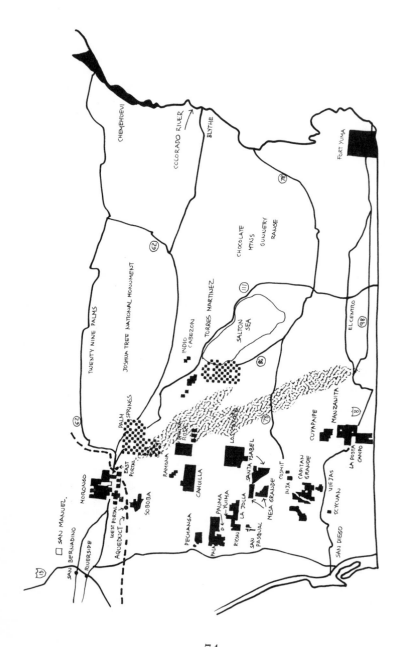

Chapter III

SOBOBA

The history of the Pit River Indians is representative of all California Indians in that all have had to struggle against whites who wanted the land. From the example, however, one might conclude that whites had a free rein in taking whatever they wanted and that this work of dispossession was confined to the wild and wooly days of early American California. The history of the Soboba Indians demonstrates, however, that there were some whites who tried to stop the dispossession of Indians and even that at times they were successful. The Soboba example also shows that dispossession can be quite contemporary.

On December 17, 1970, President Nixon signed Public Law 91-557. The publicly proclaimed purpose of the bill was published by the Senate Committee on Interior and Insular Affairs on December 2, 1970, two days before the Senate vote on what was then H.R. 3328. As the Senate Report reads:

The principal purpose of this legislation is to provide a water supply for the Soboba Indian reservation as follows:
  1. The Secretary of the Interior is authorized to approve an agreement between the Soboba Indians and the Metropolitan (MWD) and Eastern Municipal (Eastern) Water District of Southern California. The terms of the agreement in general are:
    a. Payment of $30,000 by MWD to the United States to defray part of the cost of constructing a water supply system on the reservation.

b. Concurrent annexation to Metropolitan and Eastern Municipal Water District without annexation charges (valued at $200 per acre) and, while the land is held in trust by the United States, it would not be subjected to the encumberances and taxation, and,

c. Satisfaction of the Soboba Indian's claim for damages growing out of the construction of the San Jacinto tunnel without admission of its validity by MWD or Eastern.

2. Provision is made for the United States to finance the construction of a water distribution system to deliver water within the reservation.

At a quick glance it appears that the Soboba reservation was the recipient of a fair settlement for a water dispute. Such a settlement would seem remarkable since Metropolitan Water Company is not known for its fairness. The model for the movie, "Chinatown," Metropolitan is still one of California's most powerful corporate bodies which, for example, had choked and continues to choke the economic development of the state's Owens Valley by confiscating most of the area's water and channeling it to Los Angeles. The Indians had gained from the powerful company the right to annex to the water district for no fee which meant that water would be delivered to reservation homes if an internal delivery system could be built. Metropolitan would contribute $30,000 toward the construction of such a system and the federal government would finance the rest. Seemingly the only requirement of the Soboba Indians was that they abandon all claims to damages against Metropolitan Water District and Eastern Municipal Water District, its subsidiary in the Hemet-San Jacinto Valley. Here was a chance for the United States to make partial amends for what had happened to the California Indians. The bill was passed easily and sent on for the President's December 17 signature.

How the Soboba band and the President of the United States came together on December 17 is a product of history. An examination of that history clearly shows that P.L. 91-557 was not all that it appeared to be. Soboba is a small Indian community located in the San Jacinto Valley some one hundred miles southeast of Los Angeles on the other side of

the San Jacinto Mountains from Palm Springs. Its people—
over a century fluctuating in numbers from one to two
hundred—survived when other Indian communities have
not. This survival is partly due to the fact that Soboba was
spared the first onslaught of immigrant Americans. During
the period of Mexican rule, the government gave what was
then known as the San Jacinto Valley in various grants to loyal
subjects. As with other Mexican grants, they were given with
the stipulation that land occupied by Indians was to be
excluded. On December 21, 1842, José Antonio Estudillo was
given a grant which became known as San Jacinto Viejo, and
the people of Soboba found themselves contained within its
boundaries. Fortunately for the Indians, Estudillo and his
heirs were able to maintain possession of most of their land
even after California became a state. The heirs continued to
respect the inviolate nature of Indian lands, and Soboba was
thus kept isolated from the advance of Anglo-Americans during the decades when most Indians were being dispossessed.

In 1880, however, when the heirs to the Estudillo grant
received final legal confirmation of their right to the land,
they began to formulate plans to sell the bulk of San Jacinto
Viejo. In 1882, 18,000 acres were sold to a group of American
land speculators, and one M. R. Byrnes, a businessman from
San Bernardino, bought title to 700 acres, on 200 of which was
situated the Soboba village. The days of Soboba's isolation
from trouble with Americans were over.[1]

It first appeared that Byrnes might leave the Indians
alone. Indeed he assured them that he had no desire to take
their lands and only requested that he be allowed to water his
sheep at one of the springs located in their village. Concern
grew, however, when Byrnes filed to have the land declared
his own. Still he assured the Indians that he had no intention
of evicting them and that he only desired to establish his right
to compensation from the federal government when and if
the area was included in a reservation. Byrnes was being less

77

than honest, however, and he informed the government that unless he was paid the asking price for his land he would evict the residents of the village and take possession. To support his demands, he showed up at the village with the sheriff and eviction notices. If Byrnes thought he could get money from the government, he was wrong. The government had no intention of purchasing for Indians, and Byrnes' ultimatum was ignored.

Considering what had happened to other Indians, no one would be surprised to learn that Soboba as an Indian village died at this time in history. Defenseless as the Indians were in the courts since they were not citizens with the right to retain their own attorneys, Byrnes should have been able to evict the Indians in short order. Hundreds of other villages had already been taken in much the same way. It was only by a quirk of fate that Soboba survived. At the very time Byrnes was ordering the Indians from their land, Helen Hunt Jackson, the renowned humanitarian and champion of the Indians, happened to visit Soboba and hear of the impending evictions. She not only informed her friends in the Philadelphia Indian Rights Association, but she also used her considerable political influence to force the United States Attorney General to retain the law firm of Brunson and Wells to represent the Indians. What followed is of considerable interest in that it explains the relatively unique survival of Soboba and because it illustrates the government's near total disinclination to protect Indian rights no matter how sound they might be.

Brunson and Wells quickly assumed their duties, and in 1883, the President did indeed declare a 3,172 acre tract, including the village, the Soboba Indian reservation.[2] Negotiations were begun with Byrnes and assurances were made that the case would be kept from going to trial, but this was all before word came from the Department of the Treasury that officials there did not consider payment of two attorneys for these Indians a worthwhile disbursement and refused to allocate the money. Without the prospect of recompense for their considerable effort, the two attorneys reluctantly withdrew from the case. Byrnes, despite his promises, took the opportunity to push his case to court, and the Soboba people were declared losers by default since no one was there to represent them. The mission Indian agent John G. McCallum was hardly interested in fighting Byrnes since the two were involved in real estate transactions involving Indian lands over the mountains in the desert.

Just when it seemed that the Indians at Soboba had no friends, the Philadelphia Indian Rights Association took up their case before they could be evicted. C. C. Painter, the driving force in the Association's Indian program, took the case directly to President Arthur who arranged for the appointment of one Shirley C. Ward as attorney for all the Mission Indians. Again the Department of the Treasury refused to pay a salary for an attorney representing Indians, but this time the Indian Rights Association was one step ahead. The Association's leaders, in anticipation of the refusal to pay Ward, had agreed to pay his salary if the government refused. Secure knowing that his fee would be paid, on March 11, 1886, Ward started preparation of the appeal in district court. On April 6, 1886, Indian Commissioner Atkins made it clear to Ward where the Department of the Treasury would stand and that he would get no money from the government. Officials in Washington must have been surprised when Ward continued the case with Indian Rights Association funds.

Ward's legal brief was brilliant. He clearly showed that the Treaty of Guadalupe Hidalgo gave the people of Soboba certain rights that could not be alienated. The United States Attorney General, in fact, was so impressed, that he decided to appoint Ward special counselor for the government in other land cases not involving Indians. When Painter heard that Ward would also receive a handsome retainer for this new work, he was driven to write, "It appears that it is only when the interests of Indians are involved that men are expected to serve the government for disinterested motives."

It was soon apparent that even the most brilliant brief would not win the case for Soboba in the Superior Court of San Diego. As before when it came to a choice between a white man's or an Indian's rights to land, the verdict would be in favor of the white. Ward lost. The defeat, however, was not enough to dissuade him from appealing the decision to the state's Supreme Court. A stumbling block, though, was the required appeal deposit of $3,000. Ward appealed for the money first to the United States Attorney for California and then to the United States Attorney General but was turned down in both cases. The United States Attorney General told Ward that he should abandon his interest in the case and "allow execution to issue."

Ward then approached the Indian Rights Association whose secretary Herbert Welsh responded by sending him $3,300 from his own personal funds. $3,000 was for the deposit, $300 was for Ward's salary. Ward, with the funds finally at hand, appealed the case and on January 31, 1888, the lower court decision was overruled and Soboba was saved.

Certainly the government could not claim credit for having spared the village. In fact, while these cases were in progress, the government was appropriating other land nearby. Two Indians living on lands included within the new reservation, but outside the lands claimed by Byrnes, informed the government that they wanted to obtain individual title to the land they occupied so they might not lose it as the others were apparently about to do. When they were told that it was impossible to do so they appealed to the Secretary of the Interior to have him declare the section of Indian land they occupied as public domain so that they could claim it under the homestead law. The Secretary was glad to return reservation land to the public domain and complied, but it was soon discovered that the land restored was indeed reservation land but not that which the Indians occupied. The two Indians, finding their land still part of the reservation, requested that the error be corrected, but their request was ignored, and when C. C. Painter traced the request, he found it pigeon-holed in the Bureau of Indian Affairs.[3] A clerk told Painter that the Bureau did not understand what the Indians wanted and that these particular Indians were troublemakers anyway. Not surprisingly the parcels mistakenly transfered to the public domain were never returned to the reservation.

Individuals and the government of surrounding communities still found ways to obtain desirable portions of the reservation, but the 1888 California Supreme Court decision played an important part in keeping Soboba from being dismantled in a wholesale manner. Unlike the lands on Warner's Ranch, Soboba was not attractive enough to warrant the expense of overturning a ruling of the California Supreme Court, and land was still cheap enough in the then relatively isolated San Jacinto Valley to divert settler interest elsewhere. As a result of the humanitarian flush of the early 1900's, a few acres of isolated land was added to the Soboba reservation, and until the 1930's, the Indians lived a relatively unmolested, though poverty filled, existence on a land base of slightly more than 5,000 acres. In areas where springs, streams, or wells supplied water, orchards and crops were planted, and life was at least adequate.

In early 1931, The *San Jacinto Register* began reporting on a tunnel proposed to be bored through the Valley's northern mountains in order to carry Colorado River water to a thirsty Los Angeles.[4] Such a tunnel, the paper claimed, would mean jobs for local men and some relief from the depression that was gripping the nation. The citizens of what was by then known as the Hemet-San Jacinto Valley, however, failed to recognize what it would mean to deal with Metropolitan, a company directed by unscrupulous and powerful men who put the interests of Los Angeles above everything else.

To make a long story short, the Hemet-San Jacinto Valley received nothing from Metropolitan. Local men did go to work for her in the tunnel, but conditions were so bad that the men went on strike. The company simply bored the hole with laborers brought in from elsewhere in Southern California. If all had ended there, the tunnel's history might have been forgotten.

In 1933 the company struck a major underground flow of water in the path of the tunnel's course. The water flowed as a flood into the valley. The company dammed the water until it could no longer be contained and then diverted it down the normally dry San Jacinto River. Workmen tried to seal the flow but failed and so connected the pipes and sent the water on to Los Angeles where water from this source continues to flow even to this day.

It was not long before the water tables in the valley began to drop. Springs began to dry up. Metropolitan had no rights to the water it had tapped, and because of its legal position, its attorneys began to settle with white residents. None of these individual settlements was totally equitable, and finally Metropolitan was forced to agree to supply water to the valley through a subsidiary created for the purpose, Eastern Municipal Water District.

Metropolitan, though forced to yield in some cases, brought all of its considerable power to bear against its various adversaries, and in this power struggle the Soboba Indians were perhaps the biggest losers. Virtually every spring on the reservation dried up as would most of the wells. The Indians were helpless to assert their rights because the government refused to represent them, and when they tried to mount some protest of their own, the government interfered. For instance, after being denied meaningful assistance from the government, the band, in a 1941 resolution, demanded $36,000 in settlement, but the company, with the encouragement of the Bureau of Indian Affairs and Department of

Interior, responded by denying the validity of the claim and attempting to settle with individual Indians.[5] In one case the company won a release in exchange for a used pick-up truck and a 150 gallon water tank.[6] A real settlement was not forthcoming, and by this time there was only enough water left for delivery to half the reservation through a patchwork system maintained by the Bureau of Indian Affairs. With water so severely limited, only slightly more than 100 acres could be irrigated so most of the previously productive fields became useless and many orchards were devastated.[7] The residents living on the half of Soboba left completely waterless had to haul their water from spigots of the reservation system or from the local white community.

The resultant economic loss has been immeasurable. What potential agricultural output was destroyed? How many acre feet of water has been taken? What potential production was destroyed? How many land use alternatives were eliminated? No one can know, but we can surmise that if the Sobobans had been whites and had their own attorneys, there would have been a fair settlement of a substantial amount. The Soboba Indians, however, had the Bureau of Indian Affairs.

All of this is not to say that Sobobans did not attempt to retrieve the resources that had been lost. As a band they took action on two fronts. First they tried to deal with Metropolitan directly. After Metropolitan ignored the 1941 demand for $36,000, the Indians, in 1946, had the Department of Interior, as their representative, insist that Metropolitan restore conditions at Soboba to those that had existed prior to the construction of the tunnel.[8] This was not an impossible request to fulfill. The water company could have piped water to the reservation or reinjected it back into the earth to reestablish the water table. Such action would have been expensive, however, and Metropolitan responded predictably with half-hearted and superficial attempts to comply and then with a declaration that it could and would not accede to the band's demands. The Department of Interior responded to Metropolitan's refusal to comply by dropping its demand with the cover-up conclusion that it would be impractical and impossible for the water company to bring water back to the reservation.[9] In 1954 the last irrigation water was cut off, and the remaining few acres of irrigated land joined the rest in unproductivity.[10] By 1955 the Indians were again in negotiations with a recalcitrant Metropolitan when the company tendered a settlement offer of $10,000. The Sobobans responded by demanding $100,000 and Metropolitan countered with an offer of $20,000, whereupon the band again approached the Department of Interior for help and asked that it initiate a formal suit against Metropolitan.[11] In 1956 this request was turned over to the Department of Justice which equivocated publicly saying it was difficult to assess the damages upon which the $100,000 was based. While thus weakening its bargaining position, the Department of Justice attorneys contacted Metropolitan and Eastern for an out-of-court settlement. In June 1958 Metropolitan offered the Indians $30,000 and the annexation to the water district of slightly more than half the reservation at no charge. The offer was far too low, and the Indians refused to accept it, but the Department of Interior requested that the suit for $100,000 against Metropolitan be dropped and the Department of Justice complied.

The Indians had discovered that the main pitfall in trying to sue the water companies through the Department of Interior was that the federal government was simply no more concerned about the wishes of the band than it had been in the late 19th Century. Most of the negotiations with Metropolitan were conducted without knowledge of the Indians, and when the $30,000 settlement was submitted to the band for approval, it was as a *fait accompli*. When the band refused to accept it, the government used every means to cajole a favorable vote from Soboba.[12] Government representatives

84

told the people that if they did not take the settlement they would get nothing from the water company and that the Bureau would respond to their recalcitrance by turning off the drinking water system, thus leaving the reservation completely dry.[13] Some members of the band were cowed by such threats, but most were not.

The refusal of the federal government to protect the Indians had forced Sobobans, long before the 1958 offer, to join other Mission Indians who had lost their water resources in a common action against the government. Under provision of the 1947 law that allowed Indians to present claims to the Indian Claims Commission, the Soboba band and others filed a claim against the United States government for its failure to protect Indian possession of water resources. The case, soon to be referred to as Docket 80-A, was soundly based on a principle established in the 1908 United States Supreme Court case of Winter vs. United States which established that when the United States government founded reservations it agreed with the Indians that the land and water that made the land productive would be maintained for Indian use. The Winter Doctrine, as the principle came to be known, further asserted that if the federal government failed to protect and maintain those water resources, then the federal government was liable for damages if it would allow itself to be sued. And under the provision of the 1947 law establishing the Indian Claims Commission, the government gave that permission, and the Indians took the opportunity to bring suit. Because Docket 80-A was separated from the larger California case and thus escaped the out-of-court settlement of 1964, it survived beyond the 1960's as an active case.

While Soboba was pursuing these two approaches to settlement, their possession of the land was not threatened. The irony of the destruction of Soboba by Metropolitan is that it made Soboba so totally unattractive to a local, basically agricultural community that no one thought much about taking

85

lands. The only exception of note was when the army corps of engineers took a corner of the reservation for a flood control channel. Beginning in 1960, however, retirement became an incredibly profitable industry in the Hemet-San Jacinto Valley which in turn added prosperity to local support industries, all of which allowed local entrepreneurial landholders to thrive and expand. The agricultural nature of the valley changed rapidly. Orchards were now seen as potential tracts of houses, and as happens in urban sprawl, the land's agricultural productivity became less and less important as it could support a house no matter what the condition of the top soil. Soboba came to be seen as an unused piece of real estate, and thus was born the scheme to take it from the few resident Indians. The desires of the Indians to settle their water claims became both a complication in this scheme and a vehicle for its implementation.

The government wanted the band to settle with Metropolitan and since the Bureau controlled the reservation's water supply system, it had a weapon with which to encourage the Indians to acquiesce. Finally, with this sort of blackmail hanging over their heads, the Indians agreed to allow the Department of Interior to resume negotiations with Metropolitan. In 1964 Congress passed a bill purportedly allocating $164,000 to construct a water supply system for the reservation.[14] $40,000 of that money was spent promoting and preparing for a settlement between the two water companies and the Soboba band.[15] Finally on January 17, 1965, the band agreed to accept a proposal from Metropolitan and Eastern which offered them $30,000 in damages and free annexation of the entire reservation to Eastern Municipal Water District.[16] In 1966 the young congressman for the district, John Tunney, introduced H.R. 16017 which allowed the Secretary of the Interior to approve the agreement between the Soboba band and the two companies. In its original form this bill was not a bad one. That the Indians would in fact receive the entire

$30,000 was assured by Section 1 (a) which read, "Metropolitan shall pay to the Secretary of the Interior for the use and benefit of the Soboba Indians the sum of $30,000." Section 5 assured the Indians that the government was willing to pay all that was necessary to build a water system without a concurrent claim on the Indians when it specified that, "There are authorized to be appropriated and expended such funds as may be necessary to carry out the purposes of this Act. All funds expended by the United States pursuant to the terms of the annexation and water service agreement with Eastern shall be nonreimbursable." Section 1 (b) releasing the water companies from liability for the damage caused by the construction of the tunnel was somewhat loosely written and appeared to release them from infractions they might commit in the future, but all agreed that this concession was unintentional and could be corrected with revision. The most odeous part of the bill was section 6 which read:

Nothing in this Act shall affect the rights of the Soboba Indians to pursue their claims against the United States under the Act of August 13, 1946 (60 Stat. 1049), now pending in Docket No. 80-A before the Indian Claims Commission, but any expenditure of the United States under this Act may be considered as an appropriate offset against any award the Indians might receive.

The Indians were upset with this provision as they saw the claim 80-A as quite a separate matter, but at the same time they were not certain of winning the case, and the government had promised to pay for the system even if Soboba failed to collect with 80-A. They thought they could tolerate such give-and-take if they could get the water they needed.

The Indians did not know, however, that Tunney's H.R. 16017 would be transformed from a bill designed to provide Soboba's Indian residents with water to one designed to force the Indians from the land so it could be turned over to developers. H.R. 16017 was sent to the House Committee on Interior and Insular Affairs where it remained until it died with the adjournment of Congress. Why the committee killed the bill is not entirely clear. Tunney claimed that the committee had no other choice because administrative departments refused to supply the committee with required reports. Tunney reintroduced the bill on January 14, 1969, as H.R. 3328 and the committee finally acted effecting a series of major revisions for which there has never been a public explanation. It was here that the bill became clearly defined as a piece of legislation that was not in the best interests of the Indians. The committee declared in a revised section 5 that:

Expenditures would not exceed $316,658 in addition to the unexpended balance of sums previously appropriated and available for a water supply to the Soboba reservation and the $30,000 provided pursuant to subsection 2 (c).

Not only did the committee rescind the promise made in H.R. 16017 that the government would supply all needed funds, but it also proclaimed the confiscation of the $124,742 remaining from the 1964 appropriation of $164,000 earmarked for the construction of a domestic water system at Soboba. The Indians were distressed by the proposed confiscation of their $30,000 not only because they considered it unjust, but also because the government had already laid claim to it as an offset against any settlement that might come from 80-A. The committee was taking an additional $30,000 for a total of $60,000 taken from the $30,000 award. Even more disturbing than this creative book work was the taking of the $124,742, for it meant that the Indians could not fall back on the 1964 law to obtain their water system.

Section 6, as revised by the committee, was even more specific about the government's intentions. It read:

Nothing in this Act shall affect the right of the Soboba Indians to pursue their claim against the United States under the Act of August 13, 1946 (60 Stat. 1049) now pending in docket numbered 80-A before the Indian Claims Commission, but any expenditures under Subsections 2 (c), (e), and (g), and the $30,000 paid by Metropolitan and used pursuant to subsection 2 (c), may be used by the Commission either in mitigation of damages or as an offset against any award which the Indians might receive. If such amount exceeds the award, the excess, and all expenditures by the United States under subsection 2 (c), (e), and (g) after the date of the award, shall be repaid to the United States, without interest, by deduction from revenues received by the Soboba Band or its members from the sale, lease, or rental of the lands, such deductions to be in amounts that will reimburse the United States within fifty years, or as soon thereafter as possible, according to the estimates of the Secretary of the Interior, which estimates may be revised from time to time: Provided, that deductions in any one year shall not exceed 50 per centum of the revenues received in that year.

The section reconfirmed the confiscation of the $30,000, the $124,742 and funds which might be gained from successful litigation associated with 80-A. The Indians were also notified that if the total resources from the above sources fell short of total payment, they would have to pay the difference from resources of their own—more specifically from the "sale, lease, or rental" of their lands. In other words, the Soboba Indians were, by law, now forced to pay the entire burden of a massive $371,000 water system — a system that apparently went far beyond the needs of the residents. In effect the committee was planning on saddling these poverty stricken Indians with a mortgage of almost a half million dollars. Their only chance of paying back the sum would be if they chanced to win it with 80-A. As shall be seen later, the committee did not anticipate that happening but instead projected the transfer of Indian lands to non-Indians. Thus through a revised H.R. 3328 the Indians were to be stripped of all their resources and a great part of their land in order to finance a water system that non-Indians were going to use. If there was any doubt about the committee's intention to take control of Soboba from its residents, it was ended with the addition of a new section 7 which read:

Notwithstanding any other provision of law, any assignment of land on the Soboba Reservation shall be modified, reduced in size, revoked, or otherwise limited by the governing body of the Soboba Band, or by the Secretary of the Interior if in his judgment the government body fails to act effectively in order to assure that the benefits from the development of the

89

land with water provided pursuant to this Act, other than for subsistence purposes, will accrue to the Band rather than to the assignee.

This meant that the Secretary of the Interior could take land from an individual Indian if he thought the use of that land was not conforming to Department of Interior concepts of what was proper development of reservation lands. There is no doubt about what the committee thought was the proper use of the reservation. Its report clearly states it with:

In view of the fact that water may be provided for irrigation, the committee is particularly interested in seeing that the irrigation, if undertaken, is on a commercial basis that will contribute to the repayment costs.

and with:

the highest and best use of the reservation land is for residential, commercial, and recreational purposes, if water is provided. If all of the lands were devoted to these purposes, the reservation could accommodate a population of about 20,000.

There was no talk of providing funds for the Indians to use in developing their own property and certainly the committee was not anticipating a population explosion on the reservation that would increase its Indian population to 20,000. The committee was talking about settling the reservation with non-Indians, a position even more clearly defined later in the report:

The Government will have settled its liability, if any, to the Indians through the claims litigation, and any additional cost to the Government to provide water to develop the reservation lands should be repaid from the revenues from those lands. This is particularly true in view of the fact that the reservation is to be developed for intensive residential and municipal use by non-Indians as well as Indians.

The committee never devised the outright sale of Soboba, but with the seemingly innocuous section 8 it came close:

The second sentence of section 1 of the Act of August 9, 1955 (Stat. 539), as amended (25 U.S.C. 415), is hereby amended by inserting after Gila River Reservation the words Soboba Reservation.

This added Soboba to 19 other reservations whose lands could be occupied by non-Indians by virtue of 99 year leases. The purpose of section 8 was clearly explained before the House when Congressman Wayne Aspinal amplified:

The bank is authorized to execute with the approval of the Secretary, long term leases in accordance with a 1955 act that now applies to 19 tribes the type of residential and municipal development contemplated for the reservation will require such leases if maximum benefits are to be obtained.[17]

Aspinal further assured his colleagues regarding long term development plans that the Committee on Interior and Insular Affairs:

refuses to overlook the fact that it has oversight authority in this matter and we intend to keep our fingers on the development to see that everything is carried out for the good of the tribe.[18]

The good of the tribe, of course, involved its relinquishment of land and resources. The vote was taken — yeas 287, nays 11, 2 answered present while 129, including the absent John Tunney did not vote.[19] The Senate approved the measure on December 17, 1970, to complete the transition to Public Law 91-557.

No one can rationally argue with the fact that the Soboba Indians deserve, both legally and morally, recompense from both water companies and the government. Superficially, the only apparent question is did P.L. 91-557 give Soboba enough? As one pursues the law, however, it becomes starkly apparent that P.L. 91-557 gives nothing at all. It is an aggressively dispossessive law conceived in the spirit of 19th Century California Indian policy. One finds that the real intentions of the bill are buried in its subtleties. The House and the Senate were duped into a land and resource fraud of the crassest kind with the incredibly powerful taking from the most pitifully weak.

The only step required to implement P.L. 91-557 was for the Soboba band to annex to Eastern Municipal Water District. All the water company had to do was hold hearings, and if fewer than 25% of the reservation's registered voters protested, annexation would proceed. More than 25% did protest, however, which by law forced Eastern to call an election among those living on the reservation.[20] Instead of an election among those living on the reservation, however, the total band, those living on and off the reservation, were instructed to vote in the election. And, in much the same way such tactics worked with the Pit River Indians, the vote was for annexation to the water district. In the case of Soboba, however, the election was not allowed to stand.

Eastern continued to pressure for annexation with the singleminded purpose of ending any chance the Indians might have of collecting damages for the destruction of the reservation's natural water supply. Indeed, as the years progressed the spector of a claim grew increasingly probable. In early 1976, Soboba received a favorable ruling on Docket 80-A. The court ruled that the winter doctrine was correct. The government had the responsibility to provide Soboba with water. Not only had the court recognized the damage done by Metropolitan, but it had also informed the Indians that the government would have to supply the reservation with water whether or not they approved P.L. 91-557. Agents of Metropolitan and Eastern were driven to subterfuge.[21] They issued an annexation petition to the registered voters of the reservation when it was discovered that only a few Indians were registered and that most of those favored the settlement. Only a hurried campaign on the part of other Indians to register voters opposed to annexation kept the water companies at bay this time.

The machinations of Metropolitan and Eastern certainly were not in the interests of the Indians, but they were understandable. Company officers wanted to end the Indians' claim against Metropolitan with the payment of a mere $30,000 when it had the potential of many millions. Business executives could not survive if they acted otherwise, and it must be remembered that Metropolitan hardly had the reputation for benevolent humanitarianism. It also must be realized that neither Metropolitan nor Eastern had anything to do with the alteration in the bill that made it such a vehicle for the dispossession of the Soboba Indians. As a matter of fact, the changes were as much against the interests of the water companies as the Indians because they delayed resolution of the claim. It is the various governmental agencies and those individuals who are within them who are the real villains in this episode.

Much in the tradition of 19th Century reservation philosophy, the government in its various forms used deprivation in an attempt to break the will of these California Indians. The existing well water system on the reservation was simply allowed to fall into a state of advanced deterioration. Bureau inspectors admitted that the pipes were more scale than iron and a health inspector informed the Indians that if the well were off the reservation it would be condemned without hesitation. When Indians claimed they had a right to water and demanded that the system be repaired, they were told that they could get water by annexing to Eastern. New homes were offered through the Mission Indian Housing Authority. Some were even built, but the new housing program was brought cruelly to a halt on the grounds that the new homes could not be supplied with potable water.[22] The government's interest in forcing the Indians to accept the settlement outlined in P.L. 91-557 was different from the water companies', but was no more involved in the welfare of the Indians. Not only was there a plot to take the potentially substantial settlement from Docket 80-A, but also to take the reservation itself.

It became increasingly clear that the band as a whole would never approve P.L. 91-557. The April petition ruse by Metropolitan and Eastern was a desperate move, and it turned out to be quite an embarrassment to both the companies and to local Congresswoman Shirley Pettis. It was likewise clear that since the Indian water system continued to deteriorate, there would be further embarrassment unless something were

93

done to prevent a total collapse. In April Pettis' representatives began discussions with the Indians in an attempt to find common ground on which to build an alternative approach to supplying water to homes on the reservation. The Indians quite predictably stated that they would have nothing to do with annexation to Eastern or approving any other provision of P.L. 91-557. They wanted the government to build them a new water system like that of the surrounding communities. They wanted it to be independent of Eastern supplied water, so they insisted that wells be drilled, and drilled deep enough to provide a long term water supply of adequate quantities. Finally, they did not want to see any chargebacks from the construction of the system. Federal courts had stated time and again that water on federal reservations was a government responsibility.

Pettis wanted a solution to the reservation's water problems, but P.L. 91-557 precluded any other than annexing to Eastern. In late April and early May, the congresswoman and her staff wrote an amendment to P.L. 91-557 which allowed the Indians to turn to the Indian Health Service for help. The amendment was added to H.R. 2525 which on September 30 became law as P.L. 94-437, the "Indian Health Care Improvement Act." Also included in the act was provision for the allocation of $103,000,000 over three years for the construction of water and sewer projects such as Soboba needed.

Pettis and her staff deserve credit for what they did. They set the stage for the construction of a new water system that the Indians desperately needed. Unfortunately it did not come quite soon enough because the Indian Health Service did not feel compelled to act with haste. In late June 1977 the Soboba water system completely collapsed.[23] A full half the population woke to find no water coming from their taps. The Indians ordered water trucks in from the local San Jacinto Water Company to a dry tank that could supply the waterless houses. The water and transportation bills, however, soon

94

mounted to more than the band could pay. The California Department of Forestry responded to their plight with a number of truckloads of water relying on authorization based on a mandate to respond to health hazards faced by any large group of people.

During all of this, the Indian Health Service was consistently hostile to the requests for aid and in fact blamed the situation on the Indians. Bruce Ferris, a field engineer for the Indian Health Service, said, "the band feels the solution is to buy water, but we feel the immediate solution is conservation at the lower end of the system." He also added, "more water conservation is needed there ... gardening is unnecessary at a time when some people are without drinking water." The only relief from such insensitivity came from the state of California when, in mid-July, it stepped into the breach to arrange delivery of plastic pipe to the Indians as replacement for the rotten pipe until a permanent system could be built.

Aid did eventually come to Soboba. Funds were supplied through the Economic Development Agency and through the Indian Health Service to drill a new well and build a system for the reservation. A new water system has been built at Soboba, and the band will not have to annex to Eastern and thus accept the provisions of P.L. 91-557. This respite does not obscure the fact that the reservation has been victimized by all concerned. It does not obscure the fact that a United States representative, later senator, was part of a most contemporary scheme to take an entire reservation from its occupants. Dispossession for Soboba is not an anachronism. It was very nearly today.

Pomo Indian man with a burden basket.
—Courtesy Smithsonian Institution

Chapter IV

THE RESERVATIONS

Most books about the history of California discuss Federal Indian policy and its reservation system as uniquely humanitarian in an otherwise wild and brutal California. How this view could develop, with such a mass of evidence to the contrary, is a mark of both the effectiveness of more than a century of Bureau of Indian Affairs propaganda and the gullibility of the public — historians in particular. Federal policy, with the reservation as its foundation, was never designed to help Indians. It was, in fact, designed to help the government, and a critical aspect of its function was the brutalization of the Indians of California.

By the end of 1851, most of the 75 million acres which had been Indian under Mexican rule were in the hands of non-Indians. The only exceptions were a few hundred thousand acres occupied by those Indians who had managed to survive the machinations of the first years of American occupation. Mostly these were people who had lived or resettled on land so isolated that whites had not coveted it, or on grant land whose owners still could and were willing to abide by the stipulations of the original grants. There were also small parcels amid settlements of tolerant whites. Theoretically these survivors were still protected in their rights to the land because the Treaty of Guadalupe Hidalgo accepted the Mexican principle that possession was adequate proof of Indian ownership of land. The only way to invalidate these rights was to make the Indians move. It was for this purpose that the reservation system was devised in the early part of 1852.

On March 3, 1852, President Millard Fillmore signed an act creating a "California Superintendency," and on March 4 Edward F. Beale was appointed its first head. Beale examined the earlier California reports and toured the state in mid-1852. With firsthand knowledge of the situation, he conceived of a scheme for the dispossession of all remaining California Indians, the essence of which was that reservations were to be established again, but not through treaties guaranteeing Indian possession of land. Indians were to be forced or lured to government-owned reservations where they would find themselves without the one remaining basis for any claim to California — their literal occupation of the land. With reservation Indians at the mercy of the government, reservations could be abandoned at will if whites might later want the land. This concept of reservations as moveable gathering places caught the imagination of federal officials who saw it as the solution to troublesome rights guaranteed Indians in the peace with Mexico. Once Indians moved to government reservations their ties and claim to their land would be broken, and California would at last be free of the final obstacle to progress. With an act of March 3, 1853, Congress gave Beale permission to establish five such reservations.[1] For the next half a century the government would establish and abandon reservations with almost total disregard for the welfare of the Indians involved.

Beale chose the Tejon Pass area at the southern end of the San Joaquin Valley as the site of his first reservation. The most compelling attribute of the place was its lack of fitness for human habitation. As Beale wrote:

In the "Four Creek" region, there is already a large and flourishing settlement, and this fact alone is better than all explanations I could give you of

98

the inferior quality of the land I have selected for this reservation, since every settler passing beyond has left as unworthy his labor, the tract I have indicated.[2]

There were also some indications that the land chosen was already privately owned, but permanent occupation was not part of the concept and the government was destined to eventually abandon the reservation anyway. As Beale said:

You will also observe that I have not made either treaties, or Indian reservations, nor do I propose to do so. I ask that this land may be set aside as a Government reservation, so that the Indians holding it by no other title, but the will of the Government, may at any time be removed at its pleasure.[3]

Though Beale did found Tejon and another little known one called the Wool Reservation, he proved to be a poor implementor of his own ideas. He failed to establish the other three reservations, and it is doubtful that he was even able to assemble at Tejon more than 1,000 people, some of whom were already on the land when he arrived. The Wool Reservation was never actually occupied. This lack of success, coupled with the fact that funds seemed to disappear under Beale's management, resulted in his replacement and a halving of appropriations for the project.[4]

The next superintendent, Thomas J. Henley, arrived at his post on July 27, 1854, fresh from total failure as Postmaster of San Francisco.[5] Despite the problem of a skeptical Congress created by Beale's bad example, Henley proceeded with the system as originally conceived because he thought it to be good policy.[6] Henley decided not to occupy the Wool Reservation and instead established Nome Lackee, some one hundred miles north of San Francisco. He then turned to the Indians of Colusa County who were being systematically exterminated by white settlers, and convinced them to abandon their lands and resettle on the new reservation. In November 1855 the President approved a third reservation called Klamath River located at the mouth of the Klamath River. Henley was constrained from establishing any more reservations by a still skeptical Congress, but he continued to expand by resorting to semantic fiction when he founded a number of "farms" technically attached to existing reservations. In late 1854 and mid-1855, two farms were created, one on the King's River and the other on the Fresno River. In late 1855 the Mendocino farm was established on the northwest coast, and in September 1856 a final farm was founded with the occupation of Nome Cult Valley, soon to be known as Round Valley. By the time Round Valley was occupied, however, Congress had already succumbed to Henley's success and allowed Mendocino to become a recognized reservation. Round Valley soon followed.[7]

California historians who argue that these reservations and farms were the result of government concern for the welfare of Indians do so in the face of a mass of evidence to the contrary. The truth is that disruption of Indian lives was part of a federal policy, for it encouraged Indians to look at reservations as attractive havens. The brutality of this system is beyond question. Federally supported paramilitary expeditions launched against Indians were only a small part of government operations, but they brought untold suffering. These expeditions were organized under an 1851 California law that allowed white citizens to organize "volunteer companies" to fight Indians at any time they so desired.[8] Thus, if a group of men wanted to kidnap women or children to sell into indenturement, if they wanted to collect the scalp bounty paid by various communities, if they wanted to kill for revenge or for entertainment, they organized into a California volunteer company and plunged into the interior in search of the helpless Indians. Subsequent laws added another inducement by guaranteeing daily stipends for participation in such campaigns — stipends for which the federal government readily reimbursed the state. One can imagine the chaos caused by heavily armed men, generally hostile to all Indian people, who had license to do anything they wanted to any Indian they found. Not only did the federal government pay these men, but if the fighting got rough, regular troops could be called in to rescue them and help complete what had been started, no matter how outrageous. The army commanders sometimes complained about the brutality of the volunteers, and the volunteers sometimes argued that the army did not always take necessary action against local Indians, but the two consistently worked together. They were both working for the same employer — the United States government — and this employer had one end in mind — forcing the Indians to abandon their land.

Toward the goal of dispossession, the government had one other powerful weapon besides the military: hunger. With the exception of a few bands in the low deserts of the south, Indians of California did not practice agriculture before the coming of whites. To sustain life, various foods were seasonally harvested. In Northern California, dried salmon, acorns, and various wild grains were stored for feeding people during the winter months. Without this food the people starved, but by 1853, the salmon runs had already been drastically reduced because the salmon could not survive the silt-laden conditions created by hydraulic mining of the watershed. Acorns remained for some, but the supply was drastically reduced after whites found them to be good hog food. Large stands of oaks were fenced in and porkers turned loose to graze on the acorns. Fields of wild grains became pasture for other livestock. And even where some food was still available, as in the Pit River area, military campaigns during the milder months made gathering very risky and the protection of stationary caches of food nearly impossible. When hunger verged on starvation, the objective of the government was at hand. The Indians had only three choices — to die on their land from starvation (or starvation-induced disease), to steal from local whites, or to ask the government for help. Death cleared the land, theft brought paramilitary or military campaigns that

101

resulted in death or forced removal, and help was given only after the Indians had agreed to leave their land for reservations.

If the government had truly been interested in Indian welfare, it would have offered aid to those in need. Instead, food was used as a means of dispossession just as was the military. Superintendent Henley was perhaps the most adept broker of starvation. He developed the policy of steadfastly refusing to relieve non-reservation Indians. As he wrote in response to a request to help the Pit River Indians:

Though it must be admitted that the Indians suffer immensely, and hundreds die every winter from actual starvation, I am still of the opinion that any attempt to feed them in their rancherias would be attended with a heavy expense and would result in little to benefit them.[9]

When writing of Indians who had come to Fort Jones for food, but who had refused to resettle at Nome Lackee, Henley said:

I have no doubt of the meritorious character of these Indians, but I regard the policy of feeding those who refuse to go to the reserves as injurious to the policy of colonization as contemplated by the system now in operation.[10]

And to further elucidate his policy, Henley wrote, "all Indians are opposed to removal when it is first proposed to them, but I find no difficulty, so far in getting them to the reserves as fast as I can provide food for them."[11] Throughout his tenure, Henley repeated the essence of this policy to his Washington superiors and told them that he would continue using food as a means of dispossession until someone told him not to. No one ever did. Thus, the federal government filled the reservations. They were not supposed to be havens for harried refugees. They were the essential part of a brutal policy of dispossession.

One might suppose that the government would have made the reservations pleasant places to live for those who had given up their rights to the land they had previously occupied. But the government's record on the reservations is hardly any better than its record off. Since federal authorities saw reservations only as temproary holding places for Indians, making them good homes for the Indian residents was considered a waste of money. Certainly there was little effort made to provide the promised food and security. Nome Lackee, the most utilized reservation in the early years, is a good example. Though it was packed to overflowing, Indians were still encouraged to become or were at least accepted as new residents. When a family arrived, its members were told that if they wanted shelter they would have to build huts for themselves and that they would not be fed until the agent was absolutely sure that they had consumed any supplies they might have brought with them. When the supplies were finally given, each member found that he or she was expected to live on three pounds of wheat or barley a day. Henley, proud of the economy of such short rations, proudly calculated that an Indian could be fed for as little as 4½ cents a day. Henley coldly wrote, 'I wish to make a fair trial here where no beef has ever been given to the Indians as to what extent they can subsist without it.' Twice Henley had to send troops to the reservation to avoid major Indian uprisings.[12]

Besides being victimized by Henley, the Indians of Nome Lackee were victimized by local agents as well. On March 17, 1857, Henley decided on V. E. Geiger as sub-agent for Nome Lackee. Geiger convinced the Indians to plant some acreage in grain so they would have more to eat. He subsequently had the reservation resurveyed so the planted land would be outside its boundaries, and then he bought the land and forced the Indians to harvest the crop which was sold for his profit.[13] As if this were not enough, Geiger next took advantage of the loose California indenturement laws to enslave Indians under his supervision. In partnership with another reservation employee, Geiger was able to find a local judge who indentured to them a total of 72 reservation Indians.[14] Though Nome Lackee would survive a few more years of official existence, by 1862 it was all but stripped of Indians. Its main function until abandonment was as the exclusive grazing land for the Superintendent's private herd of cattle.[15] All of this was known to officials in Washington, but nothing was done. After all, the end result was as planned. The Indians had been separated from lands which they might claim under provisions of the Treaty of Guadalupe Hidalgo.

The same government created or abetted deprivations elsewhere in Northern California. With the connivance of Henley white settlers built a lumber mill on the Mendocino reservation and workers were given food bought for the Indians. Indians were given jobs, but found they could not collect their wages. Many Indians on the reservation literally starved to death while reservation livestock, which might have saved them, was used to haul lumber to the mill.[16]

The agent on the Fresno farm ordered the Indians to forage for wild foods while he spent his time building a farm and house on a piece of property next to the reservation.[17] In 1861 the Klamath River flooded to such a degree that the entire Klamath River reservation, including animals, equipment, buildings and supplies, was swept into the Pacific Ocean. Instead of rushing supplies to rebuild and feed the suffering survivors, the Indians were ordered to move north to a small farm on the Smith River where they could better fend for themselves.[18] The Indians at Round Valley were given a daily ration of three ears of corn. The murder of reservation Indians was frighteningly common. In one incident alone, settlers, with the knowledge of the agent, killed more than 100 Ylakee Indians at Round Valley because they suspected that they were preparing to leave the reservation and feared that they might steal cattle in the process. It must be admitted that the agent was dismissed for allowing the murders, but no one was prosecuted, and whites remained free to deal with Indians as they saw fit.[19] The fate of the Indians of Northern California was well summed up by Fred Pikley, the Attorney General of California, when he wrote:

I think I can say without fear of contradiction that never were Indians so badly abused and so shamefully treated since our Government existed as these digger tribes have been in California.

It seems as though our Government at Washington has exerted itself to choose those agents who possessed the greatest ability to advance their own interests by robbing the Indians and who were most utterly destitute of any feeling of humanity.[20]

In Southern California the government showed the same disregard for the welfare of Indians. Tejon was still the focus of attention. The main function in the early 1860's was to absorb the Indians of the Owens Valley who had been removed to make way for mining operations in the area. Corruption was as rampant as in the north. The agent's cattle were numerous and roaming at will over Indian land. J. Ross Browne, an early chronicler of California, wrote, "I consider Tejon reservation little more than a private stock farm." Indians who needed government supplies were often forced to buy them with money earned from local white farmers, and local whites found that they could purchase government supplies at Tejon as well.

In 1862 a single agent, conspicuously out of tune with federal Indian policy, wrote that he felt Indian title to Tejon could be easily established if the government would employ counsel to fight a flimsy settler claim to the land. But the retention of Tejon for Indians, and the employment of lawyers in their defense was not part of policy. The government refused to fight the claim, the reservation was lost and the Indians were forced to relocate on the small Tule River Farm which had been recently established and was owned by a sub-agent of Tejon. As if to punctuate the success of the policy of evicting Indians so whites could take the land, the eventual owner of Tejon became none other than Edward F. Beale, its founder.[21] No, the reservations were not retreats for the In-

View of an Indian village near Ukiah.
—Courtesy Smithsonian Institution

dians. What they were is best summed up by one M. Frinkkum who wrote on February 14, 1862, "the reservations in this state have been the theater where the most inhumane, most shameful tragedies have been acted, furnishing the bloodiest chapter in the history of California."[22]

The Indians of California had in effect been given a second dose of the process that they had experienced with the 18 treaties. They had been convinced or forced to leave the land on which they lived and to relocate on reservations that were supposed to provide them with support and protection. After abandoning their land they found not salvation but empty promises. Without their own land there was no way for most to eat. Some survived on the reservations despite conditions, some were indentured, some settled on ranches to become virtual peons, while others fled to towns to face oppressive vagrancy laws. In retrospect, these were some of the lucky ones. Most California Indians starved to death or were killed by famine-related diseases that rampaged through Indian communities. Those Indians who tried to steal to feed their families were often hunted down like animals. The Indian population of 200,000 in 1848 had dropped to a pitiful 17,000 by the end of 1864.[23] Though federal Indian policy in California was primarily aimed at vacating the land, it was genocidal in practice, for it resulted in the rapid demise of 183,000 people.

When examining what was the California Indian policy during the remainder of the 19th Century, one must realize that, even though the decline in population was arrested, no fundamental change occurred. The government continued to use the reservations as temporary gathering places for Indians cleared from land desired by whites. In 1864 a reservation was created at Hoopa as part of a peace settlement with the Hoopa Indians who had waged a successful war against both settlers and the regular army.[24] Even as Hoopa was being established other reservations were being abandoned. California in a concurrent resolution, requested that Nome Lackee be put up for sale. The government responded by selling not only Nome Lackee, but Mendocino as well.[25]

It was not long before the government also began a campaign to terminate Hoopa. Funds for the support of the reservation were soon cut, but the government kept moving Indians onto Hoopa. In 1869, 320 Indians arrived from Smith Valley after the Smith Valley reservation had been dismantled.[26] With few government supplies, overcrowded conditions and a corrupt reservation administration, extreme deprivation plagued the people at Hoopa. To make matters worse, the agent at Round Valley wanted Hoopa abandoned and its budget reassigned to him. He convinced Washington to appoint a friend of his as agent at Hoopa. This friend, J. L. Broaddus, went to his post with the intention of sabotaging the function of the reservation. By the end of 1874 Broaddus was supported in his actions by local whites who were covetously eyeing the reservation's lands. In January 1875 federal

107

officials began to receive petitions from these people asking that the reservation be opened for settlement. On October 15, 1875, agent Broaddus received a letter from the Commissioner of Indian Affairs ordering him to remove the Hoopa Indians to Round Valley. Broaddus told the Indians that he was going to move them, and in a move quite unusual for California Indians, they told him that if he tried they would kill him.[27]

The government's tactic turned to making conditions so miserable at Hoopa that the Indians could not resist the move. Broaddus' recommendations alternated between marching the Indians to Round Valley in the dead of winter with no food, to shipping all the Indians to Indian Territory in Oklahoma from where they could not possibly find their way home. The government settled on a plan to strip the reservation of all equipment and remaining stockpiled supplies. With the Indians deprived of sustenance, they would have to move. On September 1, 1876, the Commissioner of Indian Affairs ordered Broaddus to remove the livestock and portable goods. The agent at Round Valley was ordered to help in the move, and he willingly sent a contingent of men to Hoopa to haul away the livestock and goods he wanted. The remaining goods were sold locally for a fraction of their value. As the sale was described by an army officer:

The stock, consisting of horses, mules, and cattle, have been taken to Round Valley. Such farming implements and tools as were not taken there were sold to citizens at a mere nominal sum, viz, hay from 50 cents to $1.50 per ton, while the contract from the military post is $44 per ton; wagons, thrashing-machines, reapers, mowers, etc.; in like proportion.[28]

Economics would have dictated against such a sale, but economics had nothing to do with it. The Indians of Hoopa were to be starved out of the reservation. But the Hoopas still refused to go, and the government, stinging from a costly war with the Modocs, was not willing to wage another to dislodge them.

Pomo woman seated in front of her home.
—Courtesy Smithsonian Institution

Hoopa survived because of the determination of its Indian people and because of the assistance of the army. Fort Gaston was located on the reservation and the army wanted to keep it. The Secretary of War knew that if the reservation was abandoned, Fort Gaston would be abandoned in short order. On January 1, 1877, agent Broaddus recommended that the reservation be sold at public auction despite the fact that Indians were still living there, but at virtually the same time, the Secretary of War requested that the reservation and its lands be transferred to his department. On January 5 the reservation was offered to the War Department, and on January 26, 1877, the Secretary accepted jurisdiction. With no government interference, the Indians organized a self-sufficient internal economy with the aid of local military men. Work parties were organized to tend fields, log timber and perform other jobs that bought food and money to the people. The government responded to this initiative by imposing a law which forbade Indians on reservations from working in teams without the supervision of at least one white employee. This meant that, at best, only two groups of Indians could work at one time since the government allowed only two whites to work on the reservation. When the Indians tried to get approval for the construction of a road out of the Hoopa Valley so they could ship goods to white communities, Congress refused to act on the request. In 1890 the army captain at Hoopa reported that gold had again been found on Hoopa and that the entire area would be inundated by whites except for the presence of the army. In the same year the Commissioner of Indian Affairs recommended to the Secretary of the Interior that the military be withdrawn, and it soon was. It is incredible that Hoopa survived all this relentless pressure.[29]

The small amount of success realized by the Hoopas was not to be repeated in many other localities. The demand for land by whites in Northern California continued and, unable to break up the Hoopa reservation, they sought alternative Indian lands to open up for settlement. In the process, the reservation system proved its worth. The Klamath River reservation had been abandoned since the great flood of 1861. No agent, no supplies, no protection had been accorded the Indians since that date. Then in 1879, the reservation mysteriously appeared on the official map of the Commissioner of Indian Affairs. As was to become clear, the only reason the reservation was put on the map was because the government wanted to sell the land occupied by those Klamath River Indians who had managed to stay or find their way back to their homes and eke out some meager existence there. But before that could be done, a mechanism had to be devised to establish government control of the area — thus the reservation was reborn, in name if not in fact. After allowing the reservation

110

to remain on the map for four years, the government ordered the agent at Hoopa to travel to Klamath River to inform the Indians that they would have to choose small plots for themselves because their "reservation" was going up for auction. With only slight protest from a few concerned whites, the Indians, whose people had lived along the Klamath River for centuries, found themselves confined to small plots of land surrounded by new white neighbors.[30]

If the whites wanted reservation land, it was easy enough to get. The government either made it available to them by reclassifying the land and selling it in parcels, or it simply looked the other way while farmers, ranchers or loggers appropriated the reservation lands at will. Reclassification of land almost always occurred retroactively, there being rarely any regard for the welfare of the Indians. The Indians at Tule River, for instance, lived under miserable conditions because there was not enough arable land there to support them. With full knowledge of the shortage of land, the government gave up half the reservation when a small group of whites asked to have it. Then, after it was realized that valuable timber was located on the half retained by the Indians, the agent in charge began plans to build a road into the wooded lands to facilitate whites who wanted to log it.[31]

An even better example of such accommodation to white expansion is found at Round Valley. Whites first came to the valley when the agent invited them to settle so he could have some whites for company. Taking advantage of a vaguely-written California law that allowed whites to claim the valley as swamp and overflow land when it was neither, by 1875, three quarters of the reservation land had been taken by settlers. The Indians were then moved into a more remote 102,118 acre plot much inferior in quality to that which they had once possessed. Within ten years nine tenths of the new land was also occupied by white squatters. A sympathetic agent, in contrast to the founder of Round Valley, ordered troops to re-

111

move the whites, but was ordered to desist by his superiors. Most of the land occupied by whites was lost to the Indians forever. The government's interest in maintaining the reservation withered, and it was reduced in size and then ordered dissolved altogether.[32]

In Southern California some three thousand so-called Mission Indians escaped the first two decades of this dispossessive reservation system. They were spared mainly because most of the early American interest in California had been confined to the northern gold country. But this was only a postponement, for, as the gold rush waned, interest turned to the rich agricultural land to the south. By 1870 whites were ready to dispossess the Indians in the south, and they had a well developed system to accomplish the task. In that year two reservations were founded in a remote area southeast of present-day Temecula — one in the San Pasqual Valley and the other in the nearby Pala Valley. As far as the Indians were concerned, both were poor sites for reservations because the best acreage had already been taken by 150 white settlers. As for the government, the locations were fine. The establishment of comfortable, even tolerable living conditions for Indians was not part of policy. In an articulate presentation of this policy the Mission Indian agent wrote:

I would report that, in my opinion, the Mission Indians in Southern California are retarding the settlement of that portion of the State, inasmuch as they are in possession of Public Lands which they do not and will not cultivate to any reasonable extent. Therefore, I would most respectfully recommend to the United States government to either compel them to locate forthwith on the designated reservation, in order to leave the land which they occupy open to white settlers, or to make citizens of them, to take their chances in the race of life along with the white and black races of the country.

Owners of land grants with resident Indians saw the new reservations in exactly the same way. As the agent wrote:

As far as it has come to my knowledge, there appears to be a growing disposition on the part of grant owners to eject the Indians from their lands,

112

and by many of their actions in that direction had only been delayed in anticipation that the Government would at an early day provide suitable reservations for these unfortunate people. Now that the reservations have been set apart, the grant owners have commenced moving in the matter. The Indians on the Temecula grant have been warned to leave by the 1st of September next.[33]

Everything went as planned. Indians were enticed to the reservations from surrounding public and grant lands. With this basic task accomplished both reservations were promptly abandoned.[34] The Indians scattered to find sustenance as best they could.

With the success of the first two reservations in the San Pasqual and Pala Valleys, the system was then applied in Southern California on a large scale. Between December 1875, and May 1876 President Ulysses S. Grant issued executive orders which created seventeen new reservations. The purpose was the same and whites took quick advantage of the new reservations. Executives of Southern Pacific, for example, found them essential. The government had given railroads huge tracts of land in alternate sections along their routes as a form of financial assistance and as an inducement for expanding the railroad systems. Thus Southern Pacific had acquired large tracts of land throughout the Southwest. In California, however, title to this land was questionable since much of it was still occupied by Indians. The problem was solved with the creation of the new reservations. Indians were expelled from railroad land and title secured. In the Colorado Desert, the location of present-day Palm Springs, reservations were made of sections alternating with railroad land. Thus the Indians residing on land claimed by the railroad were simply ordered to a neighboring square that had not been given away.[35]

Owners of old Spanish and Mexican grants took advantage of the situation as well. Two of the new reservations, Agua Caliente and Santa Ysabel, were located on grant land owned by ex-governor of California, John G. Downey. After

Indians had been removed from the rest of his land, he requested that the order creating the two reservations be rescinded which was done on January 17, 1880 by President Rutherford B. Hayes. With the Indians at the mercy of Downey's attorneys, the process of eviction began. In an August 17, 1880 report, Agent S. S. Lawson wrote to the Commissioner of Indian Affairs:

In a conversation a few days ago with Ex-Governor Downey, the present owner of the ranch, he informed me that he was about to sell it, and before he could give possession the Indians must be removed.[36]

Hayes added some reservations, but also eliminated others, or parts of others when powerful white interest so demanded.[37]

In some cases, as in the north, the government abandoned reservations after whites had already taken the land. In his August 17, 1880 report, Agent Lawson related that a reservation had been terminated on the Cucco Ranch in San Diego County, when the owners of the ranch forceably removed the Indians.[38] Another reservation set aside for San Luis Rey Indians was abandoned after a white filed a homestead on the land under the Desert-Land Act. He successfully claimed the land because the executive order establishing the reservation, mistakenly described its location as being in another township. The brazenness of this takeover provoked the anger of a sympathetic Lawson who wrote to the Commissioner:

How land cultivated by these people for more than a generation can be called 'desert' I am not able to answer. But it is quite likely that certain land officials in these parts who consider occupancy of land by Indians as of no more significance than their occupancy by so many coyotes will have less difficulty with such questions.[39]

The important fact to note is that this particular outrage occasioned little more than the above protest. This should be of no surprise. Protecting Indian ownership of land would have been a contradiction to the dispossessive intent of federal reservation policy in California. Thus, through the 1870's and into 1880, events in Southern California paralleled closely those in the north.

In 1880, however, it appeared that Southern California Indian history might take a different turn. Through a series of random events a group of eastern humanitarians, especially the Indian Rights Association in Philadelphia, learned of the suffering among the Mission Indians and took their relief as a project. The pressure from these people became so intense in Washington that it forced the President to appoint Helen Hunt Jackson, a famous champion of Indians, as a special agent to examine conditions among the Mission Indians of Southern California. Jackson and her assistant, Abbot Kinney, pursued their task with uncommon energy and wrote a remarkable report published in January 1884. It was a vivid description of injustice and neglect, and presented considerable evidence to support a general indictment of government policy.[40] The report concluded with a number of corrective recommendations, for which the humanitarians lobbied. Their urgings carried considerable weight, especially after Helen Hunt Jackson had published her novel *Ramona* which publicized the plight of the Mission Indians. So, unlike what was happening in Northern California, the government policy was under some public scrutiny. President Chester A. Arthur, who became president in 1881 after the assassination of Garfield, finally responded to pressure and introduced legislation incorporating all the recommendations of the Jackson-Kinney report.[41]

In spite of righteous indignation and the recommendations of Jackson and Kinney, policy and events were not to change much. The government policy that preceded the 1880's was so strong and consistent with the economic realities of the day that it had a strength that simple political pressure could not overcome, at least until the economic advantage of dispossessing the Indians had decreased. The legislation introduced by President Arthur failed to pass year after year

115

and only became law after it was clear that it would not threaten whites who held land already taken from the Indians.[42] Dispossession continued at a regular pace.

Even though the Jackson-Kinney recommendations eventually became law, their provisions were either ignored, circumvented or perverted. One reason dispossession was so effortless in Southern California was that no one knew the exact boundaries of the reservations. A white could go onto reservation land and seize it, since without specific knowledge of boundaries there was no way the Indians could prove their land had been taken. Jackson and Kinney had seen this problem clearly and recommended that surveys be ordered immediately. But this was done only in a few cases, and up until the end of the century, no agent had precise information about the size of the area he controlled, let alone its exact boundaries.[43] When a few reservations were surveyed, the result was often disaster. Surveys of the Laguna, Campo, La Posta, Inija, and Manzanita reservations showed that they were located on land other than that registered in the original executive orders, and whites moved onto the land driving the Indians elsewhere. These reservations disappeared from the list of reservations, and though they would reappear in name in the early 20th Century, they were gutted of valuable real estate.[44]

Jackson and Kinney felt that many problems could be solved if attorneys were provided for the Indians and made a recommendation to that effect which became part of the law. However, the government had no more inclination to provide attorneys for Mission Indians than they had for the Indians in the north.[45] A superintendent or agent might act from his own sense of injustice and take action against settlers who stole Indian land, but this was unusual and out of step with policy.Besides, there was always another official whites could turn to who would help them establish their claims. Even if a white had been removed from the land, it was common for him to

116

lease it back from the local agency. Many squatters simply returned to the land when the evicting agent's or superintendent's attention turned elsewhere.[46] There was so little legal representation for Indians that most owners of the old Spanish and Mexican land grants were able to force the Indians off their land with relative ease.[47]

Much land was lost without any official knowledge; local whites simply took it. Most agents did not know what was going on within their districts.[48] Again, Jackson and Kinney had recognized this problem and recommended that each agent be required to make at least two annual inspections of his jurisdiction. Though the recommendation became law, these tours were never undertaken, and even if agents had been so inclined, they were overburdened with the work of managing a huge territory with virtually no staffs. Administrative consolidation in the late 1800's for instance, left the agent for the Mission Indians responsible for a territory extending from Hoopa in the northwest corner of the state to Yuma in the southwest. Considering the size of the jurisdiction and the fact that few agents were inclined to inspect anyway, it is not surprising that a great deal of land was simply taken without any official awareness.

Jackson and Kinney had foreseen that the government might not act to protect the Indians, and they made recommendations anticipating the possibility. They argued that, with purchases of available land to augment the size of holdings, Indians could be freed from their status as wards of the government and their reservations given over to the collective body of Indians residing on them. With enlarged prosperous reservations controlled by the residents, Indians could have the financial resources to take legal action on their own to protect their title to land. Although these recommendations also became law, they were implemented no more than were the others.

By the 1880's the government agreed that the time was

right to formulate a plan to give up control of the reservations. They were no longer needed as repositories for dispossessing Indians because there were no longer any non-reservation Indians to dispossess. Those Indians not on reservations were either landless or lived on marginal land that whites did not want. The only Indian-occupied land still coveted by whites was on reservations, so the time had come for the last termination of the reservations. But to turn over these reservations to corporate tribal ownership as anticipated by Jackson and Kinney was out of the question, for it would leave some useful land in the hands of non-whites. A truly "inspired" plan developed to solve the government problems. The reservations were to be divided into various plots — some to be given to individual Indians as farms. The rest, usually the best land, was to be sold to whites. The settlers, of course, were satisfied with the plan because it would give them access to the last parcels of "unclaimed" California land. The plan also satisfied most reformers, who unlike Jackson and Kinney, had come to conceptualize a future for the American Indians as individual "white" farmers on little plots of America. Thus it was thought they could be absorbed into the mainstream of American life. All of this was experimentally applied to such reservations as Klamath River, and then it became national policy in 1887 with the passage of "an act to provide for the allotment of land in severality to Indians in the various reservations, and to extend protection of laws of the United States and Territories over the Indians, and for other purposes." It is better known as the Dawes Act. In Southern California the concepts embodied in the Dawes Act were applied through the January 12, 1891, "Act for the relief of the Mission Indians in the State of California."

It must be added that if it had not been for the pressure and watchful eyes of the reformers, it is doubtful that Indians would have been given any land at all. And to the reformers' credit, they pushed their conception of the plan to its logical conclusion, at least in California, by demanding that surviving non-reservation Indians be given their plots of ground as well. Beginning in 1893, with a $10,000 appropriation for the purchase of 330 acres of land for "digger Indians," the government began to acquire property for landless California Indians.[50] By January 8, 1927, the Assistant Commissioner of Indian Affairs could boast that 10,000 acres had been so purchased. But this did not mean that dispossession had ended as the government continued to sell large blocks of Indian land. On November 15, 1926, for instance, the agent at the Sacramento Agency accepted sealed bids for more than 35,000 acres of Indian lands. The agent at Fort Bidwell had four such sales. On December 10, 1914, he accepted bids for 25,000 acres, on October 18, 1922, for 25,000 acres, on May 20, 1924, for 25,000 acres, and as late as October 15, 1930, for 23,000 acres — all of it Indian land.

In 1933 it appeared that a significant change would occur. Franklin Roosevelt, partly at the urgings of his wife, appointed long time reformer, John Collier, as Commissioner of Indian Affairs. As Commissioner of Indian Affairs, Collier would promote a reputation that he halted, even reversed, the dispossession of Indians. In truth he was a strong opponent of the Dawes concept. He, like Jackson and Kinney before him, believed that the only salvation for the Indians was for them to attack their problems in a corporate way through their various tribes. He correctly argued that the allotment procedure had only fragmented already meager Indian resources and that poverty was forcing many Indians to sell their land to whites who had the money to develop it. In Collier's Indian New Deal of 1933, the fragmentation of tribes was brought to a halt. Even tribes dissolved under the Dawes Act were allowed to reform under constitutions approved by the Bureau of Indian Affairs. Contrary to his reputation, however, Collier did not halt or reverse dispossession. The truth is that Collier had nothing to give. Congress refused to appropriate funds

119

needed to purchase productive land, and it would not give up productive public land to Indians. Collier did add some reservations, but many of these were gained through a law that allowed Indians to return allotted land to their tribe.[52] By 1936 Collier listed 132 reservations in California. A few were huge, but most were small, many less than ten acres, the smallest a half an acre. In them all, less than 90,000 acres were of any economic use.[53] It is true that Collier saved the tribes by reforming the political structure of the reservations, but he did not reverse the dispossession that had already occurred. In fact, when the Indians of California tried to obtain reparation for what had happened, John Collier stood in their way.

Chapter V

AGUA CALIENTE
A FIGHT FOR SURVIVAL

People who have visited the Colorado Desert region of Southern California and Palm Springs in particular might think at this point that there is at least one exception to the desperate situation found on California Indian reservations today. The Agua Caliente band of the Coahuilla Indians occupy land not just neighboring Palm Springs, but within the city itself. Owning land within one of America's most exclusive resort playgrounds, the band's average per capita net worth—man, woman, and child—is more than one million dollars. Certainly the fact that this could happen is at least one bright spot in what had proved to be a rather sordid picture of white-Indian relations in other locations. But surface appearances can be deceiving. Coahuilla Indians have not arrived at their present economic status because of a history of good relations with neighboring whites, and today the find many obstacles in the way of gaining benefit from what is technically fabulous wealth.

As with Soboba, Agua Caliente survived beyond the period of the most brutal and aggressive Anglo-American dispossession. Though the Indians commanded one of the few sources of easily obtainable water in the desert, the area as a whole was so forbidding that whites simply were not interested in the land as long as other property was available.

In the 1860's Southern Pacific Railroad was granted every other section along its route through the desert as payment for building the southern transportation link between the East and West. Part of the land was occupied by Coahuilla Indians and was thus, theoretically, not the government's to give away, but, as with other Indians, the protections guaranteed by the Treaty of Guadalupe Hidalgo were largely ignored. Since no non-Indians were desirous of occupying the land at that time, little of this affected the lives of Indians. President Grant on May 15, 1876, and President Hayes on September 29, 1877, proclaimed land not already granted to the railroad to be part of the Agua Caliente Indian reservation.[1] This policy continued until the Indians had been granted, in sections generally alternating with those granted to Southern Pacific, 31,127 acres of what was thought to be mostly useless land.

Even though Agua Caliente survived the most devastating periods of American dispossession, the seeds of future destruction had already been sewn. With water, railroad access, and large amounts of land already given to a private company that would inevitably sell it, time was all that separated the Indians from permanent white settlement in the area. One John G. McCallum, agent for the Mission Indians, was the one who finally brought such settlement to the area.[2] On June 19, 1884, McCallum was appointed agent for the Mission Indians and though he proclaimed himself a champion of Indian rights, he proved he was not when on September 29, 1884, he testified to the Senate Committee on Indian Affairs that whites who had squatted on desert lands should be awarded title. On March 24, 1885, McCallum himself began to acquire what eventually would become approximately 6,000 acres for an envisaged resort and agricultural community centered on the Agua Caliente Coahuillas' water supply.[3] Although McCallum would purchase most of his land directly from the railroad, these first parcels were bought from a partnership of W. E. Van Slyke and M. Byrnes, the same Byrnes with whom McCallum as agent for the Mission Indians was theoretically locked in battle over Byrnes' attempt to lay claim to the nearby Soboba village. On October 1, 1885, McCallum left his position as agent to devote all his time and energy to the promotion of his Eden which was blossoming in the desert. McCallum's community prospered from the visits of the infirm, wealthy vacationers, and the work of enthusiastic real estate promoters. Through all of this, the Indians suffered because whites not only occupied lands the Indians considered theirs, but also commandeered water resources that were simply not plentiful enough to go around. McCallum, for instance, drilled a well in Taquitz Canyon for his own use that eventually reduced the surface flow of water from springs supplying the Indians to much less than what it had been. Even though the Indians were guaranteed a specified quantity of water from the canyon sources, that level was often unobtainable, and whites continued to find ways of diverting water for their needs. Indian agents were variably chagrined, uninterested, or supportive of water utilization by white settlers. The most positive report came from Agent Joseph W. Preston in 1888 after McCallum had built a nineteen-mile canal from the Whitewater Canyon watershed to Palm Springs. Even though the canal crossed Indian lands, Preston argued to the Commissioner of Indian Affairs that such a trespass should be allowed since the Indians could share the imported water with whites.

The decade of the 1890's, however, was one of a severe drought and water simply disappeared. It was clear, even to the most optimistic, that whites and Indians could not live together utilizing the existing systems. Both sides suffered and struggled with each other until the drought ended in the early years of the 1900's and brought temporary relief. Finally in 1911, the federal government finished a permanent and reliable water system for the area which, coupled with what came to be known as the Taquitz Creek Water agreement, guaranteed the continued existence of Palm Springs. In theory the agreement also provided for the Coahuillas by guaranteeing them the rights to the first 40 inches of water flowing from the canyon. Whites were guaranteed the next 40 inches, but only one-third of the water in excess of 80 inches. Though the Indians sometimes received 40 inches, they often did not because in times of drought whites simply diverted water from Indian canals into their own.[4]

By World War I the Palm Springs community was prospering and developers began to eye those sections of Indian land in their midst. They had every right to expect that this coveted land would become available just as it had previously in the rest of California and, for that matter, the United States. As a matter of fact, numerous Indian parcels, especially those connected with water and water systems, had already been quietly transferred into non-Indian hands. On March 2, 1917, the President responded to the needs of developers in Palm Springs and other Mission Indian areas by signing a law authorizing, even commanding, the allotment of land to individual Indians and such allotments had a past history of working extremely well in bringing an end to Indian ownership of land throughout the country.[5]

In the case of Palm Springs, however, the community was interested in more than simply ending Indian ownership of land. They wanted part of it declared a national monument as well. The area's attraction centered on beautiful wild canyons through which tourists could drive, ride horses or walk, and to insure that these lands escaped development the Palm Springs Chamber of Commerce, through its attorney, introduced a federal bill which became law in 1922, authorizing the Secretary of the Interior to acquire land from Indians and whites for the establishment of a national monument in the neighborhood of Palm Springs.[6]

In 1923 Bureau employee Harry Wadsworth was sent to Palm Springs as special allotting agent, and in that capacity he assigned parcels of land to each man, woman, and child of the Agua Caliente band regardless of whether they wanted them.[7] Some of the Indians protested that they wanted nothing to do with the allotment process, and others who might have accepted it in principle protested that Wadsworth redistributed land with no attention to its past occupancy and usage. Most also feared that after the distribution was made, the remaining 25,000 unallotted acres would be sold without their consent. With the help of such groups as the Indian Welfare Committee of the Federated Women's Clubs, the Andreas Canyon Club, the Los Angeles Chamber of Commerce, the Native Daughters of the American West, and the American Indian Defense Association (then led by the future Commissioner of Indian Affairs, John Collier) the Indians convinced the Secretary of the Interior to set aside the 1923 allotments rather than face the persistent and heavy political pressure these groups could apply.

Though the allotments had been set aside, 1924 was not an easy year for Agua Caliente.[8] Local whites demanded that the Indians fence the reservation to keep their livestock from grazing on white-owned land. These demands were outrageous considering the extensive boundaries created by the checkerboard nature of the reservation, but a number of Indian animals were shot for emphasis. Whites, especially those operating the old McCallum properties, so frequently diverted Indian water that crops failed with alarming regularity. As Lee Arenas, a Coahuilla who would later take his case before the United States Supreme Court, wrote in despair, "Year after year with new courage we plant and then our crops die in the height of the yielding season." To make matters worse, whites drilled seven wells in the general vicinity of the Indian hot springs, putting a severe strain on the only remaining reliable source of drinking water. Even the American Indian Defense Association which had helped nullify the 1923 allotments now appeared to be against the Indians. Its proposed solution for the Indian lands was to purchase them with private funds and donate them to the government for a national monument authorized by the Palm Springs sponsored 1922 enabling act. The Indians turned down meager offers of $10,000 and then $20,000 for their valuable property encompassing Palm, Murray, and Andreas Canyons and when such refusals were received with hostility, most of the Agua Caliente band abandoned all allegiance to the American Indian Defense Association and turned instead to the Mission Indian Federation for support and counsel.[9] In the meantime, government agents badgered and pressured Indians to reconsider their refusal to accept allotments.[10]

While the government pressured the Indians, their unified opposition to allotments began to wither. By the 1920's a number of Coahuillas had received enough education to think that, whatever the drawbacks of the allotment system might be, it would at least afford them an opportunity for financial gain. They felt that in comparison to other American Indians involved in this allotment process, they were in an advantageous position since a good portion of their land was part of the rapidly developing resort community of Palm Springs. The logic of getting rich on tourism and real estate was compelling even to some of those Indians without education, and feelers were sent out to see if the government would again send an allotting agent to the area. In 1927 special agent Wadsworth returned and this time he offered to allot land only to those who wished it. Under these circumstances, 24 Indians, about half the band in 1927 (including both adults and minors), chose to select parcels.[11] Each was given a 2 acre town lot, 5 acres of irrigable land, and 40 acres of dry farm land with adjustments made for Indians who preferred to have more farm land in lieu of town lots. Wadsworth presented each Indian a certificate called a "Selections of Allotment" identifying the land awarded. The certificates stated that they were not valid without the approval of the Secretary of the Interior, but regarding that approval, Wadsworth wrote assurances to Mrs. Anna Pierce about the allotment given to her daughter:

> I omitted to say in my note of today transmitting Carrie's certificate to her, that it is difficult to tell exactly when you may expect these patents from Washington, but I believe they should be here within 6 weeks or so. They will come to the superintendent in Riverside who will notify you that they are there and ready for delivery to you. In the meantime, the Commissioner of Indian Affairs in Washington authorizes me to say to you that from this date you are entitled to enter upon and take possession of these allotments, and these certificates will be your evidence of such authority until the trust patents are received by you.[12]

The other half of the band not only refused to select allotments, but vilified those who had.

In May 1927 the list of allottees was sent to the Bureau officials for review. They reported to Wadsworth that they could not approve the allotments regardless of any promises made to the Indians. As Assistant Secretary of the Interior, Oscar L. Chapman would later explain, the allotments were not approved because, "It was found that there had been included in the tentative selections for allotments numbers 16, 18, 19, 20, and 21, certain tracts of very valuable land immediately adjoint, if not actually within the town of Palm Springs."[13] The Indians were perplexed and then infuriated by this development and when offered they refused to accept alternate, less valuable parcels. With this, the Secretary of the Interior chose to review the entire notion of allotting lands to these Indians. In the ensuing years taken to consider the Palm Springs situation, the Roosevelt administration came to Washington and with it a new Commissioner of Indian Affairs, John Collier, who adamantly opposed allotments. Collier's New Deal for the American Indian proposed to rebuild the corporate tribal ownership of property, not allot it to individuals. Based on Collier's advice, the new Secretary of the

127

Interior, Harold L. Ickes, refused to approve the 1927 certificates of selection.

The band was absolutely split by the allotment issue. Half its members considered themselves progressive and forward looking because they had chosen to take land as their own. The other half did its best to argue that the allottees were no longer or never had been members of the band.[14] Each side attempted to maneuver itself into a position to control tribal government. One of the most interesting aspects of the split was the fact that neither side allied itself with the Bureau of Indian Affairs. The allottees were completely at odds with Collier because they wanted parcels of land he was not willing to give, and the others were at odds with the Bureau because they were nearly all affiliated with the Mission Indian Federation whose president Adam Castillo and advisor Purl Willis took every opportunity to criticize the Bureau and took special relish in attacking John Collier in particular.

The antagonism between Bureau and Indians was so intense that when requested to reorganize under Collier's Indian Reorganization Act of 1934, the band acted in rare concert in its refusal.[15] The split between the two factions of the band and their common antagonism toward Collier became absolute in 1935 when the allottees of both 1923 and 1927 joined with an attorney, Thomas Sloan, to file court actions to force the Secretary of the Interior to approve all past allotments. Collier responded with fury. His solitary goal from 1935 on was to dissolve the entire reservation — a stance absolutely inconsistent with the policy he established for the rest of America's Indians.

Clearly, Collier was partly motivated by vindictiveness. He proved time and again that he could be. In this case, however, he appears to have been at least equally motivated by a personal interest in the Palm Springs community. Even as early as 1924, he had worked with resort promoters to arrange the conversion of Indian lands into a national monument. In

1935 a San Diego real estate promoter had approached Collier with a scheme to lease a large part of the reservation for development purposes, and Collier was interested enough to sponsor a bill that year proposing to lease the desired land and any other the Secretary of the Interior might feel suitable for profitable development. The bill failed only because the citizens of Palm Springs opposed the bill because they felt its wording might provide the promoters with tax exempt status.[16]

Collier's actions were totally consistent with the desires of the citizens of Palm Springs. In no way did they want Indians to continue to use their lands as they had in the past. They complained that Indian projects were an affront to the aesthetics of the entire community. No one, not even Indians, denied that ramshackle buildings sat on Indian lands, most notably section 14 across the street from some exclusive resorts. Some of these homes were those of very poor Indians who simply could not afford anything else. Non-white resort workers rented others, however, and this offended the social as well as the aesthetic standards of the community.[17] Congressman Fred L. Crawford retorted in a rage when such a point of view was expressed by an attorney from the Department of Justice:

Do you think that these people, the members of the Palm Springs Chamber of Commerce, are entitled to raise a national issue simply because it happens to be that some poor people are on this land which they want to get rid of?[18]

The whites had other concerns as well. They pointed out that the continued existence of Indian land within the community's boundaries prohibited them from incorporating as a city since California law prohibited the incorporation of city governments unless all included parcels were contiguous and the attached squares of the checkerboard were not so considered.[19] Worse than this, the Indians in 1936 decided to raise the charges for going through their toll gates into the scenic Indian Canyons. The old charge had been 25¢ a car, but the

129

low fare had been abused by local resort owners who made substantial profits by running bus loads of tourists through the gates for only 25¢ each. The Indian Committee which administered tribal affairs decided to curb this abuse by raising the fare to 25¢ a car with two passengers and 10¢ for each additional person.[20] This move drove the Palm Springs Chamber of Commerce to absolute distraction and to action. Forming an Indian Committee of its own, the Chamber warned the Indians that if they did not immediately drop the rate back to 25¢ a car, it would use all its political influence to destroy the tribal government. Not only would it force a reduction of the rate, but it would demand that the Department of the Interior forbid Indians to collect any fees at all. The Indians refused to comply under such threats and the Palm Springs Chamber of Commerce did exactly what it had promised. On November 5, and again on November 13, its members sent messages to Washington outlining their complaints and presenting their demands that the current tribal government be removed and all Indian rights to collect fees be terminated.[21] At this point the goals of the Palm Springs Chamber of Commerce and those of Commissioner Collier became one, and he did all within his power to accomplish what had been requested.

At first Collier considered deposing the Agua Caliente Tribal Committee outright, but since new elections were scheduled for December 31, he decided to simply deny the band permission to hold new elections.[22] In the meantime, he ordered the local superintendent of the Mission Indians, John Dady, to choose a special agent to administer the reservations in place of the Indians. Dady chose one Harold H. Quackenbush, once an undercover narcotics and liquor agent for the Bureau in Palm Springs. On December 31, 1936, Quackenbush arrived in Palm Springs with Collier's orders.[23] From that date he would live on the reservation and would have his salary paid from tribal funds which he would collect. There would be no argument over this arrangement because no tribal committee would be elected to express those arguments. The Indians refused to cooperate with Quackenbush, but their resistance should not obscure the fact that he took absolute control of the band's finances, and with all the power of the Commissioner of Indian Affairs behind him, he had a strong if negative impact on the Agua Caliente community.

In coordination with the imposition of Quackenbush, Collier began a two pronged legislative attack on the reservation. In early 1937 he designed and introduced House and Senate bills "To Repeal that Provision in the Act of March 2, 1917 (39 STAT. L. 976), Directing the Making of Allotments to Indians of the Mission Indian Reservations, California."[24] All of Collier's future disclaimers aside, the bill was specifically aimed at the legal foundations of the Agua Caliente allotment cases pending against the government — specifically the part of the 1917 law that commanded the Secretary of the Interior to make allotments to those Indians requesting them. Some of the unallotted Indians thought the bill would help them by invalidating the 1923 and 1927 allotments thus setting the stage for an equitable distribution of reservation lands. Some of the Indians even testified in favor of the legislation, but they should not have, for Collier was introducing other bills which betrayed his real intentions. In early 1937 he arranged the introduction of Senate and House bills designed by him, with the aid of the attorney of the Palm Springs Chamber of Commerce, "To Authorize the Sale of Part of the Lands Belonging to the Palm Springs or Aqua Caliente Band of Mission Indians, and for Other Purposes."[25] Collier quite candidly testified that the bills contemplated, "the sale under conditions of competitive bidding of those parts of the reservation which are the most valuable real estate."[26] "For Other Purposes" meant the creation of a national monument from the Indian canyons. Collier freely added that if the allotted Indians lost their court cases, he would evict them and sell their lands

131

Very early photograph of a Coahuilla village.
—Courtesy Smithsonian Institution

along with the rest of the reservation. He explained that he could get a much higher price for the land if it were sold as a block, unencumbered with Indians. Congressman Thomas O'Malley somewhat incredulously summarized, "In other words, in order to make real estate valuable you will have to forfeit all tribal lands."[27] That the bills were in large part a result of the suggestion of the city of Palm Springs is beyond question in the face of open admissions that local attorneys participate in the creation of some of the legislation. Acting Secretary of the Interior Charles West eliminated any doubt when he wrote in favor of the sale of the reservation:

For a long time there has been friction between the Palm Springs Band of Indians and the residents and business interests of the town of Palm Springs. The band informally assigned to its various members the use and occupancy of certain lots on the northern part of the section which extends into the heart of the town of Palm Springs. On this land the Indian occupants erected ramshackle automobile camps and other structures which they rented and from which they derived a certain amount of revenue. However, the structures were of such character that the State Board of Health of California has been persistently demanding a clean-up, as the conditions

132

menace the health of the community . . . During the past summer and fall continued thought has been given to the matter and it has been concluded the only enduring remedy would be legislation authorizing the sale of the bulk of the Indian lands and depositing the proceeds from such sale to the credit of the band and to distribute regularly the interest accruals on the principal, reserving, however, sufficient small tracts upon which to build homes and otherwise rehabilitate the Indians.[28]

During 1937 Quackenbush, soon affectionately known as "Quack" by the white community, following his orders from the commissioner, did all he could to break the resistance of these Coahuilla Indians. Not only did he take over collection of tribal fees levied against visitors to the bathhouse and canyons, but he also began to confiscate Indian businesses. A Coahuilla, Marcos Pete, built a thriving store on land for which he had a certificate, and when Quackenbush seized the store, Thomas Sloan went all the way to the United States Supreme Court to get it back.[29] The Court issued a restraining order to the Department of the Interior whose staff took a much closer look at the situation and issued orders to Collier to have his people refrain from seizing property involved in the allotment suits.[30] They added that an Indian government would also have to be reconstituted as Department attorneys had expressed the opinion that Quackenbush's singular administration of the reservation was illegal. Though these instructions were not officially approved until November 23, Collier received them at the beginning of the month, and both Indians and Quackenbush were notified of the impending reconstructions of tribal government. With the encouragement of the Mission Indian Federation, the old Tribal Committee reformed itself and began to issue orders to stop the agent from collecting any more tribal revenue. Collier had no intention of reconstituting the obstreperous Tribal Committee of 1936 and instead ordered Quackenbush to call a meeting of the band as a whole where decisions could be made by popular vote. On November 19, 1937, Quackenbush reacted to the actions of what he considered to be a rogue Tribal

Committee by arresting its members along with their advisors, Adam Castillo and Purl Willis, on charges of embezzling tribal funds and treason against the United States.[31] Quackenbush not only arranged for individual warrants for each person arrested, but also for search warrants on their homes so he could collect the tribal records the tribe had been hiding from him. Since Adam Castillo lived in San Jacinto and Purl Willis in San Diego and the Tribal Committee members in Palm Springs, Quackenbush had to call upon numerous law enforcement agencies for assistance. He still found himself so short of help that he deputized his wife to search Adam Castillo's house. The extent of Quackenbush's arbitrary use of his authority was exposed in 1938 when he was questioned by Congressman O'Malley before the Senate Committee on Indian Affairs:[32]

Mr. O'Malley: I notice one of the charges was "treason." Do you know what treason is?

Mr. Quackenbush: Yes; I have a fair idea.

Mr. O'Malley: Well, you say. I suppose I am assuming you based your treason charge on the attempt in incite and overthrow constituted authority. Who was the constituted authority they attempted to overthrow?

Mr. Quackenbush: I was the constituted authority.

Mr. O'Malley: That they attempted to unseat and overthrow?

Mr. Quackenbush: Yes, sir.

Mr. O'Malley: That is treason?

Mr. Quackenbush: Yes, sir; that is rebellion.

Mr. O'Malley: By what section of the statute is that covered?

Mr. Quackenbush: I cannot quote it for you.

Mr. O'Malley: You are the officer making arrests and making charges and do you mean to tell me and this committee that you do not know the law under which you charge these Indians?

Mr. Quackenbush: Mr. O'Malley, I knew those things were wrong and I took it to the United States attorney and he told me what was wrong with it.

Mr. O'Malley: He found a law that would apply. Is that the way you operate? When something is wrong you go to the United States Attorney: You go to him and ask if he can find a law?

O'Malley had hit the nail on the head, not only concerning the agent, but concerning the United States Attorney as well. Agents could get help in applying even the most spurious and groundless charges.

Collier could not fault Quackenbush's arrest of Castillo and Willis because he had given the agent very specific orders to build a case against them.[33] He did, however, take issue with his having included the Coahuilla Indians, especially Francisco Patencio, the oldest and most respected member of the band. This was obviously a personal matter with Quackenbush, and the resultant bad publicity embarrassed the Commissioner and the Secretary of the Interior.[34] Collier also objected to the use of a treason charge because he knew it could not stick.[35] Willis' predecessor in the Mission Indian Federation, Jonathan Tibbet, had once been charged under exactly the same statutes and could never be brought to trial, and as a result of that case he had become a hero to the Mission Indians. Secretary of the Interior Ickes was so disturbed by Quackenbush's actions that he ordered Collier to California to defuse the situation. Collier personally arranged to have the defendants released on their own recognizance after ten days in jail under $10,000 bail. It should be added that even though Collier disapproved of some of Quackenbush's actions, Quackenbush remained agent in Palm Springs long after the arrests had been made, even after the United States Attorney dropped the case for lack of evidence.[36]

It is clear that the ferocity of the 1937 attacks broke the back of the Agua Caliente reservation. After that year there were few Indians who any longer talked about it as a reservation with a future. On the one hand was a group of allottees who anticipated the validation of their valuable allotments and as a byproduct the dissolution of the rest of the reservation. These were represented by Thomas Sloan. On the other hand the bulk of the remaining Indians, represented by Castillo, Willis, and the Mission Indian Federation, decided that since the reservation was beyond saving, their only chance to get

135

something of value was to support Collier's bills proposing the sale of the reservation. Their only qualification to that support was that the bill be modified so as to give the Indians some control over the price demanded for the property and over how the proceeds would be spent.[37] Willis told the Indians that by following this course of action they would each get a habitable house and a lifetime income of $100 per month. Neither side could tolerate the other, and congressional hearings of the time were filled with petty but violent attacks on personalities that took up literally hundreds of pages. Whites in the Palm Springs Chamber of Commerce and Bureau of Indian Affairs were adamantly opposed to allotments though Quackenbush, somewhat out of Collier's control, seems to have struck up a friendship with Thomas Sloan. The sale of the reservation was the aim of Collier and the City of Palm Springs, and they could achieve this only if they put aside traditional animosity toward the Mission Indian Federation to the point where they could have allowed the Indians even token participation in the process of dissolvement. They could not, however, and pressure from the Mission Indian Federation helped kill the bills. In 1938 the city showed its absolute disregard for Indians by incorporating and including Indian lands within the new city. There was no consultation with, let alone acquiescence of Indians.

Progress toward resolving the issues created by the 1923 and 1927 allotments had been filled with serious problems for the Indians. Resolution would come, but not without continuing a trouble filled course. The allottees received a severe setback in District Court in 1938 when their cases, by then consolidated into one known as Genevieve St. Marie et al vs. United States et al, suffered an adverse ruling. The Ninth Circuit Court of Appeals concurred in 1940, and the case was barred from a United States Supreme Court appeal because the Indian attorneys were a day late in filing. The Indians and their attorneys refused to be beaten, however, and Sloan, by then on his deathbed, arranged for new attorneys for the Indians.[38] These included John W. Preston, who had been a member of the California Supreme Court, and Oliver O. Clark, who proved to be the driving force in future legal action. Clark approached the Department of the Interior with the possibility of signing contingency contracts with individual Indians who still wanted to fight for their allotments. Assistant Commissioner Walter V. Woehlke responded that the Bureau would have nothing to do with his employment, but that if individual Indians were foolish enough to pursue the case after the Genevieve St. Marie decision, they could do whatever they wanted to do.[39] In order to reintroduce their arguments to the Supreme Court the case was refiled in the Court of Appeals under new defendants as Lee Arenas et al vs. United States. The Court of Appeals, predictably, ruled against the Indians in 1943, but on August 4, 1944, the United States Supreme Court reversed the decision and ordered the lower court to reconsider, which it did — ruling that the government had to accept the previously awarded allotments as valid.[40] With success at hand, the attorneys throughout 1944 concluded contracts to represent a majority of the Coahuilla Indians — contracts approved as fair and equitable by Judge Garrecht, the senior judge of the District Court of Los Angeles. The government attorneys appealed the Arenas decision, and in the meantime the Bureau sent one John Leytel to Palm Springs to inform the Indians that they could not possibly win the Arenas case and to vacate all land claimed under the 1923 and 1927 allotments. When the Indians failed to move within 30 days, Leytel instituted seventeen ejectment suits.[41] The final ruling on August 17, 1947, in favor of Arenas brought the ejectments to a halt, but the government would not passively comply with the court's mandate, nor would it willingly honor the contracts so casually approved by Woehlke. In a classic case of Bureau treatment of Indian attorneys, Oliver Clark was told, "you have done a whale of a

137

job, but you cannot collect a dime because we never approved your contract"—an assertion that simply was not true. When the courts ruled that Clark's contract with Lee Arenas was valid, the Bureau tried to get him disbarred for attempting to collect his fee.[42]

On February 16, 1948, Clark filed a proceeding *in mandamus* against the Secretary of the Interior to compel him to act on the 1947 decision.[43] Commanded, the Assistant Secretary of the Interior, on April 8, 1948, directed the allotment of the Agua Caliente reservation. On May 18 those claiming land from the 1923 and 1927 allotments wrote to the Secretary through their attorneys demanding that they be allotted the lands they had occupied for more than twenty years. Without acknowledging the demands, on July 21, 1948, Secretary of the Interior, Julius Krug, appointed Walter V. Woehlke special allotting agent. It was not until September 24, 1948, that Woehlke received instructions and then they made no mention of reserving lands already allotted. Land was given on a first-come basis, and as a result some Indians were awarded land that was already in the hands of others. Nor was land awarded fairly as values ranged from $27,500 to $164,740, but on April 19, 1949, the new Secretary of the Interior, Oscar L. Chapman approved what had been done.[44] Again the 1923 and 1927 allottees were forced to go to court—this time to resolve the conflicts created by the new allotments. The case was called Segundo et al. vs. United States and was later called United States vs. Pierce in the Court of Appeals.[45] The Bureau again proved itself to be a creature of habit and arranged to have Congressman John Phillips of Palm Springs introduce on May 10, 1949, another bill proposing to authorize the Secretary of the Interior to sell the reservation with or without Indian consent.[46] The bill was defeated only when Oliver Clark quite by chance heard of its existence while on a business trip to Washington. He went to the House and offered his testimony before the House committee hearing on the bill and convinced the members that the bill was designed without the Indians' knowledge, let alone their consent and that it was against the Indians' best interests. Thanks largely to his effort the bill was not reported for a vote.

On August 9, 1956, the Court ruled against the 1923 and 1927 allottees in United States vs. Pierce. The decision stated that the Secretary of the Interior did not have to honor the 1923 or 1927 allotments. What appeared to be a defeat was not, however, certainly not for the Coahuillas who were now free of the major source of disunity that had plagued them for more than twenty years. It is important to note that this reconciliation was much easier by 1956 because there were only a handful of people still living who were interested in asserting their old claims, and the few who were could no longer command much political force within the band since its population had grown from fifty to more than a hundred members, most of whom were looking for a contemporary solution to future needs.[47] The court provided a solution for all the band when it added to its decision that the allotments made in 1948 and approved in 1949 had not been fair to all members of the band and that even though the government might not be obliged to follow the exact boundaries of the 1923 and 1927 allotments, all Indians would have to receive land comparable in value to all others and that this had not occurred. The Department of the Interior would have to rectify the inequities, and if some Indians had to be given huge tracts of improved lands to equal the value of city lots already awarded, then so be it. In fact, the Department of the Interior soon discovered that the only way to meet the court mandate was to distribute most of the reservation to those band members not already awarded enough property. The court ruling brought an end to any real chance to fulfill the Bureau's and City of Palm Springs' desire to sell the bulk of the reservation to private developers and for a national monument.

It is clear that the Coahuillas living at Agua Caliente owe

Thomas Sloan, Purl Willis, Adam Castillo, Genevieve St. Marie, Lee Arenas, C. P. Segundo, Genevieve Pierce, Oliver Clark, and even John Collier and the city of Palm Springs a great deal of gratitude, not necessarily so much for what they accomplished, but for tying up the disposition of the 31,000 acre Agua Caliente reservation until a time when a court could conceive of giving it to its Indian occupants. This more than any other factor explains the present status of the band.

Even though the Indians had clearly won, federal authorities fought the 1956 allotment equalization order with determination. They resisted partly because of a traditional disdain for awarding large tracts of land to Indians, but more importantly they resisted because the order conflicted with a new federal Indian policy aimed at terminating all federal services in California as expeditiously as possible.[48] To embark on this path of "termination" the government had to avoid implementing the newly mandated allotments, for they called for continued federal involvement until such time as the Indians would be deemed capable of handling the complexities of property management. Thus it became necessary for the Department of the Interior to stall in reply to the court's mandate until such time as they could effect a strategic withdrawal. In 1957 the congressman representing Palm Springs, D. S. Saund, was asked to introduce S. 2396 which, like the bills in 1937 and 1949, proposed the sale of the entire reservation.[49] The bill was so obviously in conflict with the 1956 court decision that it seems clear that it was merely a stalling tactic. It was so without merit that the Indians easily convinced Saund to withdraw his active support of the bill and let it die in committee.

Allotment was forstalled by these conflicts until September 21, 1959, when H.R. 8587, a derivitive of the Indian sponsored H.R. 5557, was signed to become Public Law 86-339 and mandated the equalization of Indian land holdings in conformity with the court ruling. The law appeared to be what the Indians had been asking for. With the exception of Indian-owned hot springs, cemeteries, and sacred ground in local canyons, all the lands were to be allotted to the 104 members of the band alive at the time of its signing. The value of such lands given each Indian would be a minimum of $335,000.[50] Since a majority of the Indians were minors and some of the older adults were senile and obviously unable to handle their own affairs, section 4 of the law provided that the Secretary of the Interior should see to it that they be provided with guardians before allotments were made. This provision gave the Secretary authority over some Indian estates, but few complained as guardians had already been appointed in cases where parents had scandalously sacked the estates of their children, and children of their senile parents. Under California law other adults were protected from the application of Section 4 by a provision that guardians could not be imposed on adults without proof of insanity or incompetence — conditions that require explicit proof.

The government got what it wanted as well. Though allotted Indian lands were to be held in trust prior to delivering unrestricted title to the Indians, the management of these lands was to be transferred to the capable individual Indians and to guardians supervised by the Superior Court of Riverside County through its division in Indio, the community neighboring Palm Springs. As it turned out, the deal was better for the government than for the Indians. With the supervision of the allotments in the hands of the Superior Court at Indio, the government was free from administrative responsibility as was envisaged by the "termination" plan. But the Bureau burdened the Indians with an administrative replacement that was not only oppressive, but expensive beyond anyone's expectations. In one of its last acts before turning over administration to the judge in Indio, the Bureau issued a ruling that the guardianship provision in section 4 placed the Indians under the California Conservatorship Law established in 1957. Under this law the Superior Court judge could take management of property from an adult Indian and give it to a conservator if he deemed the Indian in need of assistance in managing his affairs or that he was subject to "artful or designing persons."[51]

As the situation developed, it became apparent to the Indians that P.L. 86-339 was a boon to the local Palm Springs community, not to the Coahuillas. The presiding judges in the Indio Court, over the course of ten years placed 92 of the 104 estates under guardians or conservators.[52] Though some of the minors were put under the guardianship of parents, most of the estates came to be run by non-Indians. Not only did administrative fees provide substantial revenue for parts of the non-Indian community, but also it took management out of Indian control. The guardians and conservators quickly proved their worth to Palm Springs by agreeing to clear the asethetically repugnant low income rentals out of section 14 in the middle of town.[53] They also agreed to lease the lands belonging to their wards for periods so long that they were tantamount to ownership. This was made possible through a September 21, 1959, amendment to the Indian leasing act that allowed the Secretary of the Interior to approve 99 year leases on Indian lands owned by the Agua Caliente band — the same bill Soboba would join if its members voted for annexation to Eastern Municipal Water District.[54]

The Indians protested, not only about the existence of guardians and conservators, but also about the corruption involved in the real application of P.L. 86-339.[55] In its own self interest the Department of the Interior did not pursue complaints about the arrangement. The House Committee on Government Operations did investigate, however, and on July 5, 1962, William L. Dawson, Chairman of the committee wrote to the Secretary of the Interior, Stewart Udall, suggesting extensive irregularities in the function of the guardian-conservator system in Palm Springs.[56] On August 13, 1962,

142

Udall responded to Dawson that his staff would look into a few of the charges, but caustically added:

On the other hand, it is with considerable regret that I find it necessary to dissent from your apparent view of Federal responsibility concerning the other matters mentioned in your letter. In my judgment it would be highly improper for an executive agency of the Federal establishment to generally investigate or otherwise question the integrity of State judicial administration. The estates of Palm Springs Indians are administered in the same manner, under the same laws and through the same judicial officers as would be the case for any of the other 16 million citizens of California whose affairs become subject to court supervision. This is entirely consistent with the general objective of bringing the Indian population into the framework of American society.

On August 22, 1962, Dawson responded to Udall stating that he was looking forward to the investigation, but added that, "we believe that the hands-off attitude of the Department with respect to the other items in the July 5th letter is not well advised." Following this letter, on July 9, 1963, John Carver, Assistant Secretary of the Interior, submitted a report to Dawson and the committee stating that the Department of the Interior investigation found that the committee's findings were mostly incorrect and that the guardianship-conservatorship system was functioning smoothly and fairly. Complaints continued to arrive, however, from Coahuilla Indians and from personnel in the Bureau's office in Palm Springs. In 1965 a Resource Trust Officer was appointed to work out of the Bureau's offices in Palm Springs to informally monitor the actions of the Superior Court.[57] Relations between the Bureau and the court remained amicable until 1967 when Bureau officials questioned the actions of the court's Judge Merrill Brown who was in the process of selling a parcel of his own land to an Indian estate and paying to a conservator fees which the Bureau thought exorbitant. The hint of a scandal was added when it was revealed that the conservator was also the man who was handling the judge's real estate transaction. Judge Brown responded on April 11, 1967, by

143

barring Bureau officials from reviewing or commenting on matters in his court which involved Indian conservatorship or guardianships.[58] This order prompted Homer B. Jenkins, Director of the Bureau's Palm Springs office, to request a meeting with the Regional Solicitor of the Department of the Interior, Charles R. Renda. After reviewing the facts, Renda felt compelled to investigate, reporting his findings on May 12, 1967:

As a result of the forgoing, I have concluded that the Palm Springs situation has again reached the crisis state and, in my opinion, is in need of immediate attention and action by the Department to forstall what may soon become a public scandal reflecting adversely not only upon the Department generally but upon the Solicitor's office if we fail to act in these circumstances.[59]

Faced with impending scandal, Udall ordered a special task force investigation of the Palm Springs situation. In March 1968 the Palm Springs Task Force submitted its "Report on the Administration of Guardianships and Conservatorships Established for Members of the Agua Caliente Band of Mission Indians, California." In his introduction to the report, Udall not only summarized the appalling conditions the task force found in Palm Springs, but also partially admitted to the role he played in the situation. Udall wrote:

This report and the conclusions reached therein have my full support.

The principal conclusion is that the present guardian-conservatorship system has been intolerably costly to the Indians in both human and economic terms and that it must be replaced or radically revised.

A review of the contents of the report leaves no doubt as to the soundness of this conclusion. In all frankness, I must say that I am appalled that the state of affairs described in the report has not only existed under ostensible state and federal supervision; it has flourished. . . .

The Task Force also found that a share of the responsibility for the present state of affairs in Palm Springs rests on the shoulders of this Department. When questions and complaints concerning the administration of these guardianships and conservatorships were first raised several years ago, we placed too great a confidence in the probity and ability of the state judiciary to exercise proper control and supervision over court-appointed fiduciaries and attorneys. As you know, I took steps to rectify this error a year ago.

144

Many would claim that the task force's main aim was to divert attention from the Secretary's responsibility in the matter, but whatever the truth of such charges, anyone who read the report joins with Udall in being appalled by the situation it describes.

The task force reported that of 84 estates examined, the administrative fees were 44 per cent of ordinary income excluding the sale of lands, and that among other things, two men between them had collected $485,000 from handling Indian estates. Since there were no formulas for attorney's or fiduciary fees, these matters were settled in court. The report adds that "in the Indio court this means practically automatic approval of fees requested by fiduciaries and their attorneys in Indian estates unless objections are made." The task force also found that some of the exorbitant fees were duplicates of others collected for the same services. Even the integrity of the judges was questioned. The report concluded that Judge Hilton H. McCabe has used his position and influence to become executor of various Indian estates for which he received more than $19,000 as remuneration. The report noted also that Judge McCabe had made it known that he did not favor advising Indians of their rights to nominate persons of their choosing as conservators and guardians. The task force added that Judge McCabe seemed to be involved in serious conflicts of interest and recommended an investigation. Judge McCabe eventually became a Justice of the State Court of Appeals and his successor was Judge Merrill Brown. Brown's previously mentioned misconduct and his reaction to criticism brought on the task force investigation.

A large number of attorneys, guardians, and conservators were singled out for special attention by the task force which found rampant conflict of interest, fee-splitting, sloppy and fraudulent accounting, double fee charging for a single service, and general corruption. The task force took special exception to the organization of the "Association of Conser-

145

vators, Guardians, and Allottees of the Agua Caliente Band of Mission Indians." Judge McCabe had suggested it be established in 1962 and even levied an assessment of .1 per cent of the assessed value of each Indian estate to support it despite the fact that no Indian participated in the Association. Its main function was to support and protect the guardians and conservators, and it frequently acted in direct opposition to the will of the band that bankrolled it. Though the Association was ostensibly organized to promote the development of Indian lands, funds were often used for other purposes. For instance, the Association retained an attorney to defend the organization and its members against the charges made by the task force.

The task force report pointed out that the Indians were extremely dissatisfied. They knew little about their estates, and when they tried to consult their conservators or guardians about them, they were generally charged for the time. They felt they had never been informed of their rights, and that little effort had been made to train them in administering their estates, and that there was little to indicate that the guardian-conservator program would come to an end. Guardians became conservators automatically when minors reached their majorities. In 1951, 21 out of 104 Indians were allowed to administer their own estates. By 1968, seventeen years later, this had changed to only 23.

Aside from drawing a general picture of corruption, the task force laid the ultimate blame on the federal government. The report asserted that even if anyone had been honest, the system would have failed because it was poorly conceived since the courts simply were not equipped to serve the function assigned to them in this situation. The task force did make some mistakes, and its government immunity allowed it to freely make charges that were not totally substantiated, but the overall picture was correct and the conclusion that the system was rotten was irrefutable. Millions of dollars of resources had been turned over to a court unable to oversee the individuals who were in turn appointed to administer the funds in the court's name. The temptation was more than some individuals could withstand.

Everyone at the federal level agreed that the Equalization Act would have to be revised, especially section 4 that had authorized the creation of the guardian-conservator system. On October 16, 1967, even before the task force published its report, Congressman Tunney responded to the impending scandal by introducing H.R. 13516 which proposed to keep the guardian-conservator system, but give it more mandatory safeguards through the supervision of the Department of the Interior.[60] The Indians protested. In Tribal Council Resolution 846 of 1968, the band publicly demanded the abolition of the system altogether, and with the publication of the task force report, they had enough clout to convince Tunney to submit another bill calling for just that.[61] On May 14, 1968, Tunney submitted H.R. 17273 with the support of the band, and on October 17, 1968, it became law as P.L. 90-597. Supervision of the Agua Caliente band was now back in the hands of the Secretary of the Interior.

The Coahuillas' problems were not over. The City of Palm Springs, not ready to give up on its aims, entered into a zoning war with the band. After equalization, the city fathers had not discarded the notion of preserving the area's beauty by keeping Indian land vacant. Even before the Indians had gained control of their allotments, the city council gave the Indians a warning of things to come with a general plan approved in 1965 which rezoned some of the allotted, but unleased land to less density and others to open space.[62] In 1966 the United States Attorney General was able to assert that though city zoning laws could be applied to allotted and leased lands, they did not apply to allotted unleased lands as well.[63] Nearly simultaneously, however, the Secretary of the Interior maintained that he could zone Indian lands in accordance with city ordinances if he deemed such action proper. Much to the chagrin of the Indians who anticipated a thorough and profitable development of their lands, that is exactly what the Secretary did.

After the demise of the guardian-conservator system in 1968, the Indians went to court and then tried to reach a compromise with city officials over the future development of their lands, but the city replied in 1973 with an even stricter general plan that outlined extensive open space zoning for undeveloped Indian lands.[64] Section 14 of the city, for instance, was changed from R-4 zoning, the highest density allowed to one that only allowed eight units per acre.[65] The Coahuillas did not leave the matter to the discretion of the Department of the Interior or the City of Palm Springs, however, as the Indians brought the issue of the applicability of local zoning ordinances to Indian lands into federal court. In November 1976 the Ninth Circuit Court of Appeals ruled that California cities and counties could not enforce their zoning ordinances on reservations.[66] This was technically a moot question for the City of Palm Springs, since the Secretary of the Interior had already directed it not to apply its zoning laws to the Agua Caliente reservation. Palm Springs had been party to the case, however, because it feared that an adverse decision could destroy its cozy relationship with the Secretary of the Interior in which he implemented zoning laws on the city's behalf.

Indeed Palm Springs had something to worry about because on June 20, 1977, the Department of the Interior announced that it intended to give control of zoning on undeveloped Indian lands to the Indians themselves.[67] Palm Springs responded on June 29 by declaring a moratorium on all building within the city. The city manager, Don Blubaugh, stated to reporters that "the situation posed by about 125 Indians having so much influence in a city of 30,000 permanent residents and another 15,000 part-time residents is a hard pill to swallow."[68] Hard pill or not the moratorium was a desperate move of limited potential duration as multi-million dollar projects throughout the city were brought to a halt. For the first time in four years the City Council and Tribal Council met, and after a number of meetings, on July 26, 1977, an agreement was reached in which the Council agreed to lift its moratorium for 120 days to give both sides time to reach a permanent agreement.[69]

The Palm Springs Indians may have a bright future. Certainly it would be absurd to deny that some are prosperous by any standards. The land possessed by each member of the band in 1959 was valued at $335,000. By 1977 this had increased to more than $1,000,000. Such economic standing, unfettered now by guardians and conservators and temporarily by zoning laws, has to have political clout. When the city manager complained about the influence of these 125 individuals, he failed to add that together they commanded more than $120,000,000 in real estate assets even with most of their land still undeveloped. One would hardly expect such statements to be made about such people as Bob Hope, Frank Sinatra, or Gerald Ford, even though they command more influence in Palm Springs than the average citizen. One can also surmise that statements like that will be less and less common as the city comes to the realization that Indians are no longer under its control, and as Indian economic and political influence begin to converge. Certainly the Agua Caliente band has no reason to display any good will for either local, state, or federal governments. If the members of the band do finally gain complete command of their wealth, it will be due to their own efforts to keep what was really given to them unintentionally. The local, state, and federal governments have done everything possible to rectify the mistake. Whether they will succeed is still open to question.

149

*118-year old woman from near the San Luis Rey Mission in the entrance
to her Tule reed hut.* —Courtesy Smithsonian Institution

Chapter VI

THE GREAT CALIFORNIA PAYOFF

Despite the effectiveness of the reservation system in dispossessing the California Indians, those who survived the 19th Century still had an irrefutable claim to ¾ of the state or 75 million acres. Their ownership of this much land had been guaranteed in the Treaty of Guadalupe Hidalgo, and these guarantees had not been eliminated despite the wishful thinking of non-Indians who occupied the state. Federal policy in the 20th Century was aimed at clearing up the legal contradiction created by the fact that most of California was not occupied by its rightful owners.

That it took so many years for the government to deal with these staggering legal questions was not a result of federal disinterest, but arose instead from a fear of having to resolve these questions in a court of law, for up until 1901 it was clear that if the issues were presented to a fair court, the Indians would win. So, when the Court of Claims was created in 1863, Indians were forbidden access to it, and as an added measure, the government did all in its power to keep Indians from retaining their own attorneys who might start pressing dangerous issues.[1] The situation changed in 1901 when the United States Supreme Court gave the government the upper hand it needed to deal with Indians in court. In that year the owners of Warner's Ranch in Southern California—the old

Downey property—were able to confirm in the Court their right to evict Indians from three villages located within the ranch's boundaries.[2] Though the Indians in this case had clearly occupied the land longer than whites had been in California, and thus under Mexican law, owned it, they were ordered evicted because they could not produce paper title to their land. The Justices of the Court had denied that citizens of the United States had to respect the Spanish and Mexican system that recognized Indian occupation of land as proper title, and thus, they declared inoperative the provisions of the Treaty of Guadalupe Hidalgo regarding land claims. With precedent thus established, the government became willing if not eager, to let California Indians into court for a final settlement because with the treaty officially contravened they were certain to lose.

The irony is that it was the humanitarians who were to bring the Indians to court at this inauspicious time. By 1901 an increasing number of whites were protesting past injustices perpetrated against Indians. Even before the turn of the century there had been some public rumblings about the treatment of Indians, with the Indian Rights Association and the Sequoia League being the most active of the interested groups. After researchers on an unrelated topic accidentally discovered and publicized the 18 treaties in 1905, these rumblings became an outcry. Such groups as the Commonwealth Club, the Indian Welfare Committee of the Federated Women's Clubs, the California Indian Rights Association, Inc., and the Women's Christian Temperance Union all agitated for economic aid for California Indians.[3] Speakers such as John Collier carried the same message to clubs and community organizations throughout the country.[4] At first these organizations and individuals pressed mainly for legislation mandating a Congressional appropriation for direct financial aid for Indians. Such an appropriation, however, was opposed by the powerful Director of the Budget who had absolute veto

152

power over money drawn from the general fund. He announced that if Indians were to get aid it would have to come from another source.[5] As more than a decade was wasted with no aid for Indians, the humanitarians became convinced that the only logical alternative was to turn to the Court of Claims whose awards were not drawn from the general fund. Thus the interests of the humanitarians and the government began to converge in that both wanted to clear away obstacles previously placed between the California Indians and their day in court.

Unfortunately for the California Indians, the humanitarians proved once more that good intentions do not always produce good results. The only way the Indians could gain access to the Court of Claims was through a special act of Congress, and the nature of that bill would determine the rights given Indians in court. The humanitarians, for the most part unpracticed in the art of political maneuvering and without sufficient clout, allowed the government to bully and cajole them into accepting a bill that was not in the Indians' best interests.

In the beginning the humanitarians submitted bills that would have given the Indians a chance to get just compensation for their claims. The first came in 1920 with the introduction of the Raker Bill which would have allowed the Indians to retain their own attorneys and sue the government for a sum they thought equitable. This provision allowing the Indians to retain their own attorneys was especially frightening to the government. Bureau studies were showing that the Supreme Court decision of 1901 was based on very weak grounds and might easily be overturned by a good lawyer arguing before a Supreme Court whose make-up had changed appreciably since 1901.[6] In the process, such a lawyer could very conceivably establish the government's culpability and win a huge award for the Indians. To win the support of congressmen in its opposition to Raker's bill, the Bureau informed them that if

the Indians were able to establish a just claim, it would amount
to an award of perhaps $100,000,000 and that this was, in its
opinion, neither deserved by the Indians nor affordable by
the government.[7] To avoid the wrath of Indian supporters,
the officials of the Bureau avoided a general public explanation of their real concerns, and took the position that the
Indians of California had no legal claim to the land because of
the 1901 decision. They followed with the argument that to
allow Indians to spend money on attorneys when there was no
case to win would be in violation of the Bureau's responsibility
as protector of the Indians.[8] As a result of lobbying by the
Bureau, the Raker Bill and a number of similar ones were
defeated.[9]

As difficult as it might be to believe, the humanitarians
came to believe the explanation given them by the Bureau of
Indian Affairs, and instead of fighting the Bureau, they began
to cooperate and work with legislators to develop a plan that
would satisfy the government. Finally both sides agreed in
principle to the procedures to be followed in admitting the
Indians to the Court of Claims. The government was willing to
promise aid to the California Indians if it could be sure that
three conditions would be met. The award would have to be
small — perhaps a few million, but certainly nothing close to
the $100,000,000 a just settlement might bring. Secondly, the
payment of such an award would have to be gratuitous (paid
without admitting responsibility for past wrongs) because if
the government were forced to accept culpability it might set a
dangerous precedent for other Indian claims cases. Finally, if
the Indians accepted the award, the settlement would have to
end forever all claims by California Indians. In essence the
government was willing to admit the California Indians to the
Court of Claims and was willing to give them a small amount
of relief, but only on the conditions that they refrain from
putting a serious case before the Court. This was the agreement reached between the humanitarians and the govern-

ment, but a serious problem still remained. No matter how predetermined the process and the outcome, attorneys were needed to conduct the case through the Court of Claims. Private attorneys retained by the Indians were out of the question, however, because they might not cooperate with the scheme, and so the problem was solved when congressmen from California suggested that their attorney general could argue the case. In accordance with the proposal, the California legislature in 1927 passed an act that allowed the state's attorney general to bring suit in the Court of Claims as soon as federal enabling legislation allowed him to do so. To this the Congress responded by passing the 1928 California Indian's Jurisdictional Act.[10]

The 1928 act was everything the government could have asked for. It forbade the participation of any attorneys other than those associated with the California attorney general. That there would be a small settlement was insured through a number of provisions in the bill, the most important of which consisted of a provision mandating that the case be based on the 18 treaties which the Senate had refused to ratify. This diverted the basis for suits away from the legitimate 75 million acre claim to an unsupportable assertion that the government owed the Indians retribution for not ratifying the 18 treaties in 1850 — a claim that had no basis in law. To further insure that the final award was kept small the act also stipulated that no more than $1.25 an acre would be awarded as repayment for land which had been taken.[11] These limitations were totally arbitrary and certainly not based on the real losses suffered by the Indians. As a Department of the Interior report explained:

The Bill is designed to afford only a modest amount of relief as will take care of their most essential needs. We believe that is the practical obligation we owe now. So we have in effect arbitrarily reduced the claim in behalf of the Indians. Instead of claiming for the 70,000,000 acres of land we claim only for the original estimated value of the treaty lands, we claim only at a rate of

155

$1.25 an acre. This means in effect the claim is only 12½ cents per acre for the lands the Indians originally surrendered.[12]

To the land claims the Indians would be allowed to add reimbursement for supplies and services promised in the 18 treaties. Even with this last provision of the act, the total payment for land, goods, and services could have amounted to no more than $17,000,000, but even this amount was too large for the Bureau.

Officials at the Bureau were able to further add a provision to the bill that stipulated that from the total of any future settlement the Indians would have to reimburse the Bureau for its expenses incurred between 1852 and whenever final settlement was achieved. The only goods and services exempted from this provision were those promised in the 18 treaties and which had later been delivered. After the Bureau was reimbursed the attorney general of California would be allowed to collect for some of his expenses. The offsets, as these liens were called, amounted to $12,000,000 leaving the Indians with only $5,000,000 from the original $17,000,000. Even the $5,000,000 might just as well have been ordered paid as offsets, for the act mandated that the final settlement be turned over to the control of the Bureau.[13] No thought was given to distributing the money to the Indians themselves. So in the end, any settlement won by the plaintiff would be paid to the defendant. Here was a settlement the Bureau could support.

Thus the government provided the Indians of California with "a day in court" in which, for around $5,000,000 they were to give up claim to most of California, a claim admitted to be worth at least $100,000,000 in 1852 land values — billions in those of 1928. Though the details of the act were openly discussed in hearings, the government still had the audacity to proclaim the proposed settlement just and equitable.

Some Indian leaders, most notably those associated with

the American Indian Defense Association, Inc., were fooled by proclamations about justice and equity. Others, especially in such groups as the California Indians, Inc., and the Mission Indian Federation, were not. They knew, for instance, that the attorney general of California could not diligently work for them. He represented two clients with conflicting interests — the Indians of California on the one hand and the rest of California's population on the other. Since his future was based on the support of the latter, he could never have withstood the political clamor that would have been created if he fought for the Indian claim to three quarters of the state.[14] These Indians also understood the inherent problem of discontinuity in being represented by an attorney who could be changed with every election.

When the Indians tried to amend the 1928 act in order that they might engage their own attorneys as participants in the suits, they were vehemently opposed by state and federal governments. The attorney general of California was so opposed to the participation of outside attorneys that, for two years and seven months, he refused to add certain essential amendments to his case simply because the need for them was brought to light by the attorneys of the California Indians, Inc. When the Mission Indian Federation insisted that some of its members had information vital to the case, the attorney general refused to take their testimony.[15]

The Bureau of Indian Affairs continued to argue that outside attorneys were simply out to steal money from the Indians. These arguments were so effective that the Bureau's position came to be supported by some of the most important white humanitarians and Indian leaders. It even got the once-respected California Indian Rights Association to parrot the argument. Mrs. Stella Von Bulow, a key figure in the association for many years, erroneously testified that if private attorneys were allowed to participate in the case they would take fifty percent of the award from the Indians.[16] Even the eminent John Collier became convinced by the Bureau that the Indians could get nothing more than the gratuitous settlement outlined in the 1928 act, and that if private attorneys were allowed to participate they would simply consume most of what was already a small award.[17] Thus persuaded, Collier, after becoming Commissioner of Indian Affairs in 1933, vigorously fought to exclude private attorneys from litigation on behalf of California Indians.

What many people knew, however, and what many private attorneys pointed out, was that new counsel could force an abandonment of the formula outlined in the 1928 California Indian's Jurisdictional Act and then fight the 1901 Warner's Ranch Supreme Court decision. Even if counsel collected fees the money for the Indians would be greatly increased. Collier was repeatedly reminded of this possibility.[18] In one memorable exchange before Congress, ex-senator Marion Butler, a famous Indian attorney and by far Collier's intellectual superior, forced the Commissioner to admit that an undeniable claim could be made by California Indians to 75 million acres. Collier, frustrated by Butler's attacks gave the uncharacteristically straightforward answer that if attorneys did establish such a claim they could still find the Congress standing in the way of such an award, and if by some quirk of fate attorneys could get an appropriation bill from Congress, then President Franklin Roosevelt would certainly veto it.[19] These predictions proved academic, however, for despite a long list of bills in favor of allowing private attorneys to join the suit for the California Indians, none became law.

Without their own attorneys of record, many Indians turned to attorneys or other influential men who were willing to advise them. The government, especially the Bureau of Indian Affairs, considered these men a threat as well, for they often helped the Indians write bills which conflicted with the government's position. As a result, many of these men faced severe government harassment. Some were prosecuted for

158

such crimes as interfering with the Bureau by organizing Indians or for illegally collecting money from Indians.[20] Commissioner Collier was especially successful in fanning animosities among humanitarian groups.[21] Attorneys for the Indians of California, Inc., spent as much time fighting the Indian Rights Association as the government. Still these men and women continued to draft bills and have them introduced through sympathetic legislators. The Bureau fought and defeated nearly every one of them.

The one element of the act of 1928 that *really* distressed Indian leaders was that pertaining to the size of the proposed award. It was to be so meager that, in response, there was considerable agitation to change the formula of recovery. Bills were introduced and plans formulated to increase the acreage liability — if not to 75 million acres, at least to somewhere around 17 million acres. This was justified on the dubious grounds that the men who negotiated the 18 treaties had intended to negotiate many others.[22] But, of course, basing any settlement on the 18 treaties was tenuous at best. All bills introduced to change the formula were resisted vigorously by the government because they could have imposed a larger settlement than the government was willing to pay and because it was feared that such a change might establish legal precedents for Indians in other parts of the country who were at the same time struggling with the government over land claims. F.D.R. expressed this point of view quite candidly on June 20, 1936, with a message that accompanied his veto of the only bill of this type to pass both the House and the Senate. As he said:

It appears from the report of the Senate Committee on Indian Affairs relative to the bill (S. Rept. 709 74th Cong., 1st sess.) that the total area for which an award might probably be made under terms of this legislation would be not less than 90,000 acres. Thus the bill involves a liability of at least $100,000,000.

In addition to having the effect of imposing a very heavy financial burden on the Government, the bill would create a dangerous and undesirable precedent for similar endeavors on the part of the present decendents of other aborigines to secure payment for lands occupied by their ancestors at the time of the original settlements in the United States or the acquisition of territory by this country. Not only would such a course of action result in an incalcuable financial burden to the Government, but justice to the Indians today does not seem to require this type of reparation.[23]

When the Indians and their supporters found that the struggle to change the formula could be effectively stalled by the government, they narrowed their efforts to an attack on the inequities in the proposed offsets to be subtracted from the final settlement. The entire offset structure seemed vulnerable to criticisim and change. For instance, the government used two systems for evaluating the worth of Indian land. It will be remembered that the Jurisdictional Act stated that when Indians were to be reimbursed for land taken by whites, the land could be valued at no more than $1.25 an acre. But some of this land had been repurchased by the Bureau for reservations, and for this Indians were charged offsets as high as $25 an acre. And offsets did not take into account continuing dispossession. 66,000 acres of land in the Owens Valley had been acquired for an Indian reservation and an offset of $1.25 an acre was claimed against any final settlement.[24] In 1932, however, the land was transferred back to the public domain, but the offset was never removed from the books and was, in fact, subtracted from the final award. The inconsistency was rectified in the 1960's as a result of the Indians' attempt to occupy the land for which they had been charged. Rather than let the Indians occupy the land, Congress passed a bill refunding the $1.25 an acre to the California Indians.[25] All the offsets for land were especially unjust anyway, since by June 30, 1918, the government had sold public lands—once Indian lands—for $23,000,000. Offsets for goods were as unjust as those for land. Millions of dollars of supplies were subtracted with inadequate or no accounting. But the most disturbing aspect of the offsets was that the act included a provision that bureau expenses would continue to be added to the offsets until settlement was reached.[26] By June 30, 1940, it was estimated that the offsets had surpassed the possible settlement by more than $2,000,000.[27]

The Indians, by asking for the elimination or limitation of offsets, were not asking the government for a great sacrifice. No monumental settlement would have resulted, nor would any far reaching precedents have been established, but the government still resisted. It wanted the Indians to receive some sort of settlement, but not a large one, and the offsets played an important part in keeping it small. The government held to a pseudo-legalistic argument that allowed for little alteration. As Commissioner Collier calmly explained, the government was willing to pay for promised but undelivered goods and services, but at the same time the government was obliged to the American people to charge as offsets the goods and services not promised but delivered.[28] This convenient legal explanation seems empty when coupled with Collier's statement in other quarters that the whole proceedings was a rigamarole. Contradictory as it was, this position kept the government in a relatively unalterable position. The only significant change came during negotiations for a final settlement when a small final award was already assured.

Though the government fought continually to keep the final payment relatively small, it maintained from the beginning that the eventual settlement would be *just and equitable*. But in 1936, the United States Supreme Court, in a peripherally related case (the Shosone Tribe vs. the United States), ruled that *just compensation* meant not only compensation but also interest on that compensation from the time the injustice was committed. In 1937, Indian representatives tried to take advantage of the Supreme Court decision by drafting and introducing a bill to amend the 1928 act to add the words just and equitable, the phrase the government had been using in conjunction with the bill since its inception. In response the government simply stopped using the phrase and insisted that

161

the bill must be defeated because it could lead to an award that was beyond its willingness to pay. The attorney general of California, U. S. Webb, the attorney for the Indians, was quite vocal in support of the later position.[29]

After the Indians had lost all major attempts to have the 1928 Jurisdictional Act changed, and after they had accepted the inevitability of a small award, they still persistently argued that they should at least get the money themselves and not have it turned over to the Bureau. This desire became stronger when it became clear that others had eyes for the money. In 1935 the State of California through its legislature demanded $2,000,000 from the impending settlement on the grounds that it wanted to set up its own Indian program. This demand would be repeated at least four times in later years.[30] The Indian appeals were ignored. It was commonly said that Indians were not mature enough to handle their own money.

In 1944 the futility of all opposition to the nature of the 1928 act became obvious. Then Attorney General Robert W. Kenny of California and the federal attorneys decided to bring the California claims to a conclusion. An obstacle to settlement, however, was that by 1944 the offsets had mounted to a sum far surpassing the possible award. Unless some adjustments had been made, the settlement would have had the Indians paying the Bureau for taking their land. Everyone knew that even the most callous public would not tolerate such a situation, so the government agreed to a compromise. The offsets for the reservation purchases would be calculated at a low $1.25 an acre instead of as much as $25 as originally planned. In this way Kenny and federal attorneys reached a settlement that paid the Indians instead of charging them. The settlement came to slightly less than $5,000,000 — almost to the dollar what had been estimated in 1928.

To be fair to Kenny, it appears that he had a strong feeling for the injustice of the settlement and through his last minute negotiations he established a foundation for future claims.

Gaining one of the few major concessions in nearly twenty years, Kenny managed to obtain federal acceptance of the position that the Indians whose ancestors had not signed any of the 18 treaties would be allowed to file a separate suit even though they would share in the original settlement as well. It was assumed by both the attorney general and the Bureau that the non-treaty Indians could be expected to file for the same small gratuitous settlement. Federal officials accepted the compromise because they thought it would lead to a quick settlement and an end to the claim of the Indians.[32]

There was good reason for the government to seek an end to Indian claims in California. Looming on the horizon was the possibility that the government could not maintain control of the California situation. On December 8, 1941, in a decision settling a case filed for Arizona's Walapai Indians, the United States Supreme Court made a number of far-reaching rulings. Some would be used against Indians in the 1970's. But in 1941 the Indian cause was bolstered by a clear Court ruling that Indian occupation of land also gave them title. As the Court stated:

If it were established as a fact that the lands in question were, or were included in, the ancestral home of the Walapais in the sense that they constitute definable territory occupied exclusively by the Walapais (as distinguished from lands wandered over by many tribes), then the Walapais had "Indian title" which, unless extinguished prior to the date of definite location of the railroad in 1872, then the respondent's predecessor (Atlantic and Pacific Railroad Company) took the fee subject to the encumberance of Indian title . . . Indian right of occupancy is considered as sacred as the fee simple of whites.

The underpinnings of the rationalization for the "rigamarole" of 1928 were being eroded as the Court began to question some of the assumptions of the 1901 decision.[33] The way was opening for the Indians of California to file for compensation for the wrongful loss of most of California. It is little wonder that the government was willing to settle in 1944. It must have been disconcerting to Washington when the non-treaty In-

Two Pomo Women cracking acorns outside their home.
—Courtesy Smithsonian Institution

dians, who had been freed to file their suit, refused to accept a small gratuitous sum and instead turned to the new Supreme Court decision as the foundation of their claims.[34]

It appeared that this time things would be different. By 1944, the government and the courts were facing up to the contradiction of on the one hand, proclaiming Indians as citizens with full rights while on the other, denying them the right to private counsel. For the first time the California Indians were allowed to hire their own attorneys and have them recognized by the court. In 1947 President Truman signed an act which created the Indian Claims Commission whose purpose was to settle remaining Indian claims.[35] But everything was not quite what it seemed. While the government had been forced to admit the legitimacy of some Indian claims, it still had every intention of fighting to keep any Indian settlement as small as possible. The era of duplicity was not over.

All concerned clearly understood that the type of attorney retained by Indians would make a tremendous difference in the size of the award demanded. Therefore, the Bureau turned its attention to manipulating the Indian-attorney relationship. In the name of wardship responsibility, the Bureau insisted it had to examine and pass on any attorney the Indians wished to retain. The justification for this wardship stance was questionable at best. The offsets of the 1944 settlement had not only paid back the Bureau for more than 90 years of operation, but had bought back all the land and buildings on the reservations as well. One advisor to the Mission Indians would later go so far as to argue that the 1944 settlement should have ended all Bureau influence over the Indians of California, since after that date the reservation system should have ended. But the Bureau maintained its presence on the reservations as well as its determination to control the kinds of attorneys the Indians would hire. Any attorney who decided to work on Indian cases also had to deal with the Bureau.[36]

This does not mean that the Bureau was totally successful in controlling private attorneys. Having private attorneys, no matter how carefully selected by the Bureau, made a great deal of difference to the Indians. Especially in the late 1940's and 1950's when the Bureau had not yet discovered a way to effectively control them, these attorneys managed to eliminate some of the more outrageous injustices. One early accomplishment was to get the money awarded in 1944 away from the Bureau and into the hands of the Indians themselves. After unremitting pressure, especially from the representatives of non- reservation Indians who knew money controlled by the Bureau would not benefit them, an act of May 24, 1950, ordered the Bureau to make a list of California Indians so that the money could be distributed individually among them.[37] It should be no surprise that the Bureau collected $245,000 from the settlement as payment for making the list, but by June 30, 1955, most of the remaining money had been distributed. Unfortunately the impact of the victory was nullified with the disbursement of funds to individuals instead of tribes. Each eligible Indian received only $150 which was not enough for any meaningful relief.[38]

More importantly, a group of attorneys decided to break with the constraints imposed by the government's contention that Indians had no title to land unless it was documented and confirmed under provisions of the 1851 act "to ascertain the private land claims in the State of California." The Indian attorneys presented a case before the Indian Claims Commission in which they proved that under terms of the Treaty of Guadalupe Hidalgo Indians owned the lands they occupied when the United States assumed sovereignty over California. They further showed that forcing or tricking Indians from their land did not necessarily destroy that title for the Indians involved or their heirs.

Here the government's resistance stiffened. It could not counter the Indians' case, however, and instead argued that the attorneys represented the California Indians as a whole and that the case was thus improper since only identifiable tribes or groups could present cases to the Commission. This position was upheld in court so individual tribes and bands were forced to contact new attorneys of their own who in turn had to pass the screening process established by the Bureau.[39] While suits were proliferating, however, the attorneys who had originally filed for all the Indians of California appealed the lower court ruling and obtained a reversal. In its decision the court commented on the government's duplicity by pointing out that from 1928 to 1944, Washington was perfectly willing to recognize the Indians of California as a group when such a position coincided with the government's needs. The attorneys then proceeded with their original case but without the Indians who had retained their own attorneys during the appeal. The Bureau then responded by ordering the Mission and Pit River Indians to withdraw from the case as well. Bureau officials justified the orders with the explanation that these Indians would have a better chance of winning if they were separated from the case involving California as a group. In reality this was an attempt to cripple the larger case by severing its strongest parts.[40]

Even with such underhanded maneuvering, it appeared as though the government's position was hopeless. In 1959 the Indian Claims Commission ruled that the Indians of California still had a legitimate claim to 64 million acres west of the Sierra Nevada.[41] But at this time the impact of the government's manipulation of the attorney-client relationship became evident. Indians were forbidden to pay normal attorney's fees. Remuneration had to come from a statutorily limited percentage of the final settlement. The attorneys could clear more money by making an early, smaller settlement than by spending what promised to be an enormous amount of time fighting a long and costly court case. There were 72 hungry attorneys working on the California case, and when the government offered an immediate but drastically reduced settlement of 29.1 million dollars, they accepted. They would get 2.6 million dollars from the settlement and the Indians were left without a ruling on the legitimacy of their non-paper title to California. The only stipulation made by the attorneys was that the government help them regain the representation of Indians who had separated from the case.[42]

There followed a series of actions demonstrating just how cynical and devious the Bureau could be. It will be remembered that when it appeared that the attorneys pressing the California case had an unassailable claim to a huge award, the Bureau insisted that the Mission and Pit River Indians withdraw from the case. When the attorneys of the California case decided to settle for a paltry sum, however, the Bureau had a miraculous and instant change of heart and wanted the Mission and Pit River Indians to rejoin the case. Bureau officials returned to these Indians and told them they should rejoin the suit filed for all California Indians. They were told that to do so was likely the only way they would ever get reparation for their loss of land. The Mission Indians, evidently unaware of the Bureau's scheme, overwhelmingly voted to rejoin the suit. The Pit River Indians, however, recognized that they had a very strong independent case and held a tribal council voting not to rejoin. The Bureau, unhappy with the vote, ordered the Pit Rivers to vote again, and this time absentee ballots were delivered by Bureau officials to Indians who had not voted in the first election — many with only miniscule amounts of Pit River blood and not recognized members of the tribe. The second election resulted in a slight majority voting to rejoin the case and with much protest that is just what they were forced to do. There were a few suits that could not rejoin the California case, among them the Mission Indians who kept some issues separated as did the Indians who had claims extending from California into neighboring states as well. The attorneys for the California case allowed these exceptions and quickly concluded the case. In 1964 for a claim worth hundreds of millions, perhaps billions, the attorneys and the government settled on the figure of 29.1 million dollars.[43]

There was resistance. The Mission Indians cried foul when they realized that they had given up a potentially valuable claim for a small part of an insufficient settlement. They tried to organize another election to undo what had proved to be a terrible mistake, but since they had freely voted for the mistake, the government easily blocked a new election in court.[44] The Pit Rivers began to battle to invalidate the second election and prove their right to the land, but they would also ultimately lose.[45] The Indian Claims Commssion showed some signs that it would not accept the out of court settlement. Attorney General Robert Kennedy put pressure on the Commission not to go to trial. Part of this campaign included a

168

famous article in *Life* which viciously belittled Indians and their right to reparations.[46] The Commission finally agreed not to go to trial, and in 1968, a law was passed which allowed the Bureau to take $325,000 of the settlement money for preparation of a list of eligible Indians so that this second settlement could be distributed to individual Indians. Even this money was slow in getting to the Indians. The $324,000 had been spent by 1972 with no roll completed.[47] Finally in December of 1972, the Bureau announced that it would mail awards to 69,000 recipients — a figure that included individuals with only the most minute amount of Indian blood. 6,000 would receive only $26.33, mostly their share of the $83,000 plus interest paid for the 66,000 acres that had erroneously been offset from the 1944 award. 63,000 people would receive $668.50 as their share of both the 1944 and 1964 settlements. Many Indians have refused to cash the checks, while others cashed them reluctantly because it was the only money available to buy food and pay bills.

In no way could the actions taken under the Jurisdictional Act of 1928 or the Indian Claims Commission of 1947 be considered justice. In the first case the defendant hired the attorney for the claimant and then defined for that attorney the nature of the case right down to the dollar value of the settlement. Every effort was made to insure that the settlement was kept small, and in this the government was totally successful. In the second case the Indians were allowed to retain their own attorneys, but the government was able to control them, first by obtaining veto power over those retained, and secondly, by keeping the potential remuneration of the attorneys small so they would find it economically advantageous to settle claims quickly. All of this was done in the name of justice, but was really done for expediency. The truth was that the wolves were tending the sheep.

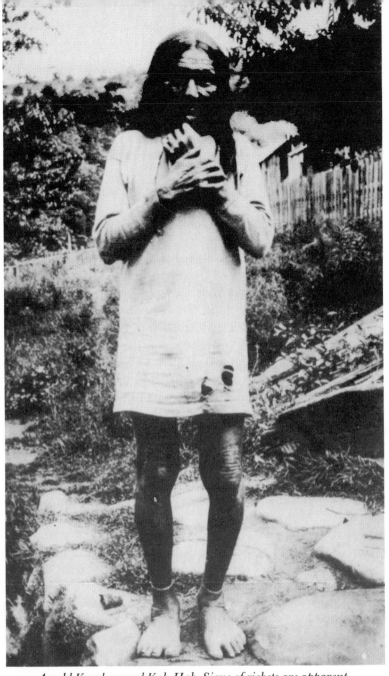

An old Karok named Kah-Hah. Signs of rickets are apparent.
—Courtesy Smithsonian Institution

Conclusion

What has transpired and continues to transpire at Agua Caliente, Soboba, and Pit River country repels anyone with sensitivity. Events clearly conflict with those principles of justice and fair play Americans claim to stand for as a people. Keep in mind that the three case studies are random samples comprising only one percent of the present population of California Indians and that today's survivors, statewide, are only two percent of those living in 1848. Extrapolating the limited picture to the larger one is horrifying.

Horror is natural and acceptable as long as it does not lead to aimless breastbeating which helps no one, and as long as it does not result in an attempt to impose short term aid at the expense of solving the long term problem, the ownership of the land. The example of the humanitarians of the early twentieth century should be enough to dissuade even the most naive. The Bureau of Indian Affairs besieges us with proclamations claiming better health, housing and education for Indians, but this should not obscure the fact that the issue of land ownership remains today much as it was in 1848. The federal government is good enough at trading food for land, or in the case of Soboba, water for land, and it does not need our assistance in doing so. Focus on the fact that the California

171

Indians have an irrefutable claim to three quarters of the state. A more startling conclusion is difficult to imagine, but it is true, and no amount of legal or public relations obfuscation can any longer hide the fact. The federal government took that much land from the California Indians in absolute defiance of the law and gave it to the state, private companies and individuals. Reparations and settlement for this loss is what the Indians need, not charity.

Some will argue, of course, that the dispossession of California Indians is long past and that the issue of land ownership is dead, killed by the passage of time, if not by law. As the Agua Caliente, Soboba, and Pit River examples demonstrate, dispossession is still quite contemporary and in fact involves real estate of greater value than that in 1848.

Even if we accept the fact that we have inherited most of the problems of Indian claims and that they are by and large not of our own making, we cannot ignore them because to do so does not relieve us of their burden. Generations of Californians have been saddled with flaws to land title that should have been settled by those who came before them. California, as a matter of fact, will not be the first state where title insurance is refused when the possibility of preemptive Indian title presents itself. In Maine this made interesting news. In California it would send economic shock waves across the nation.

One might also argue that whatever the rightful claim, we simply cannot afford to settle with the Indians. This is the kind of reasoning that has left us with a mountain of undemocratic laws and legal decisions that are now the foundation of Indian/non-Indian relations. Americans are forced to accept and rationalize the existence of a repressed people denied due process and their democratic rights. The saddest part of this approach is that none of it changes the sound basis for land claim. All it does is make a larger claim for future generations. A claim that probably could have been settled by

Franklin Delano Roosevelt for $200 million is now astronomically larger.

How much is California worth? How much income has been derived from the land since 1848? If the courts mandate an honest settlement for the California Indians, the rest of us had better hope that enough good will exists between us that they settle for less than what is due. We have a choice of dealing with this situation now, fairly and equitably, or of following precedent and passing it on to future generations until one comes along that is forced to accept judgment or is more responsible than we are. This last statement may seem harsh, and possibly it is, but it also explains the truth. The problem will not go away if ignored. It simply gets worse with time. The issue of the land must be resolved or it will explode. The California Indians deserve an honest day in court. Let them have it before it is too late for us all.

Chapter Notes

Chapter 1

1. The main sources for the history of the Pit River struggle in the 1970's were the *Inter Mountain News,* a weekly paper published in Burney and the Sacramento *Bee.* Other information was gained from the court cases themselves and the documents associated with these cases.

2. For a summary of the early history of Pit River-white relations see, W. N. Davis, *Sagebrush Corner: The Opening of California's Northeast;* Earnest R. Neasham, *Fall River Valley: An Examination of Historical Sources;* Erminie Wheeler-Voegelin, *Pit River Indians of California.* These three books are part of the Garland series, *American Indian Ethnohistory,* edited by David Agee Horr. One needs to be careful when using the above series because it is mostly composed of material gathered by the government. Erminie Wheeler-Voegelin, for instance, is one of the government's best known historians. Also see various publications of the Fort Crook Historical Society; Robert Heizer's, *Destruction of the California Indians;* Reports of the Commissioners of Indian Affairs; Record Group 75, Letters Received.

Chapter II

1. There is a great deal of disagreement about population figures. C. S. Goodrich, citing A. L. Kroeber, says that in 1769 there were between 150,000 to 200,000 Indians in California. C. S. Goodrich, "The Legal Status of the California Indians," *California Law Review,* 14 (1926), 3; S. F. Cook agreed with Kroeber in his earlier works, but later revised his figures upward. S. F. Cook, *The Conflict Between the California Indians and White Civilization,* S. F. Cook, "The California Indian and Anglo-American Culture," in *Ethnic Conflict in California History,* Charles Wollenberg, ed., 23-42, S. F. Cook, "The Destruction of the California Indians," *California Monthly,* 74

(December, 1968), 15-19, S. F. Cook, *The Population of the California Indians, 1769-1970.* Cook clearly shows that most of the deaths during the Spanish period were caused by diseases; Dr. C. Hart Merriam says the population in 1769 was 260,000, C. Hart Merriam, "The Population of California," *The American Anthropologist,* N.S., 7 (1905), 594-606; William H. Ellison estimates that the population was between 150,000 and 260,000 in 1769 and claims that in 1846 it was at least 100,000 to 125,000. William H. Ellison, "Federal Indian Policy in California, 1846-1860," *Mississippi Valley Historical Review,* 9 (1922), 38; Woodrow Borah says that there were 200,000 Indians alive in 1846, Woodrow Borah, "The California Missions," *Ethnic Conflict in California,* Charles Wollenberg, ed., 3-22.

2. Department of the Interior, Bureau of Indian Affairs, *Estimates of Resident Indian Population and Labor Force Status; By State and Reservation:* March, 1973.

3. For a good summary of Russian activity in California see, California Historical Society, *The Russians in California.*

4. For a good summary of English activity in California, see Richard Dillon, *Siskiyou Trail; The Hudson's Bay Company Route to California;* and Erminie Wheeler-Voegelin, *Pit River Indians of California,* 6-20.

5. If the "Black Legend" were not so ingrained in the popular historical literature, there would be no need to pursue this theme. For anyone unconvinced by these few pages, I refer them to the following works. John Francis Bannon, ed., *Indian Labor in the Spanish Indies;* Coy, P. E. B., "Justice for the Indians in Eighteenth Century Mexico," *American Journal of Legal History,* 12 (Jan., 1968); David Davidson, "Negro Slavery in Colonial Mexico 1519-1650, *Hispanic American Historical Review,* (August, 1966), 235-253; Charles Gibson, ed., *Attitudes of Colonial Powers Towards the American Indians;* Charles Gibson, *The Aztecs Under Spanish Rule. A History of the Indians of the Valley of Mexico 1519-1810;* Charles Gibson, *The Black Legend: Anti-Spanish Attitudes in the Old World and the New;* Charles Gibson, *Tlaxcala in the Sixteenth Century;* J. H. Parry, *The Spanish Seaborn Empire;* Philip Wayne Powell, *Soldiers, Indians, and Silver;* Philip Wayne Powell, *Tree of Hate: Propaganda and Prejudices Affecting United States Relations with the Hispanic World;* William Taylor, "Land and Water Rights in the Viceroyality of New Spain," *New Mexico Historical Review,* 50 (July, 1975), 189-212; Eric Wolf, *Sons of the Shaking Earth.*

6. Charles Hale, *Liberalism in the Age of Mora, 1821-1853.*

7. See footnote 1.

8. *Ibid.*

9. For a summary of the development of English theories of imperialism and how these theories affected English relations with Indians, see Felix S.

Cohen, "The Spanish Origin of Indian Rights in the Law of the United States," *Georgetown Law Journal,* 31 (1942), 1-21; Vince Deloria, Jr., *Of Utmost Good Faith;* Richard Schifter, "Indian Title to Land," *American Indian,* 7 (Spring, 1954); Wilcomb E. Washburn, *Red Man's Land/White Man's Law.*

10. Wilcomb E. Washburn, *Red Man's Land/White Man's Law,* 31.

11. There are numerous works dealing with early United States Indian policy. Vince Deloria, Jr., *Of Utmost Good Faith* and Wilcomb E. Washburn, *Red Man's Land/White Man's Law* are two of them. Also see Francis Paul Prucha, ed., *The Indian in American History* for a fine collection of articles. An article not included in Prucha's book, but still exceptional is one by Joseph C. Burke, "The Cherokee Cases: A Study in Law, Politics, and Morality," *Stanford Law Review,* 21 (February, 1969), 500-531. For a discussion of the history of the Supreme Court, a useful book is Charles Warren, *The Supreme Court in United States History.*

12. Letter of Secretary of War Eaton to Cherokees, April 18, 1829, and President Jackson's First Annual Message to Congress, December 8, 1829, both in *Documents in United States Indian Policy,* Paul Prucha, ed., 44-48; Joseph C. Burke, "The Cherokee Cases: A Study in Law, Politics, and Morality," *Stanford Law Review,* 21 (February, 1969), 500-531.

13. See the various articles printed in Paul Prucha's, *The Indian in American History* and in Louis Filler and Allen Guttman, eds., *The Removal of the Cherokee Nation: Manifest Destiny or National Dishonor?* Also see Joseph C. Burk, "The Cherokee Cases: A Study in Law, Politics, and Morality," *Stanford Law Review,* 21 (February, 1969), 500-531.

14. A number of works discuss the Trist Mission. See Geoffrey P. Mawn, "A Land-Grant Guarantee: The Treaty of Guadalupe Hidalgo or the Protocol of Queretaro?", *Journal of the West,* 14 (October, 1975), 49-63; Pletcher, David M., *Diplomacy of Annexation: Texas, Oregon, and the Mexican War.*

15. Al Hurtado, "Controlling Native American: California Indian Relations During the Mexican War," an unpublished paper, 1976.

16. Referring to the promises to respect Indian rights, article IX reads, "The Mexicans who, in the territories aforesaid, shall not preserve the character of citizens of the Mexican Republic, conformably with what is stipulated in the preceding article, shall be incorporated into the Union of the United States and be admitted, at the proper time (to be judged of by the Congress of the United States) to the enjoyment of all the rights of citizens of the United States according to the principles of the Constitution; and in the mean time shall be maintained and protected in the free enjoyment of their liberty and property, and secured in the free exercise of their religion without restriction." More specifically article XI reads, "The sacredness of this obligation shall never be lost sight of by the said Government, when provid-

ing for the removal of the Indians from any portion of the said territories, or for its being settled by citizens of the United States; but on the contrary special care shall then be taken not to place its Indian occupants under the necessity of seeking new homes, by committing those invasions which the United States have solemnly obliged themselves to restrain." To allay any concerns the Mexicans might have had about the final form of the treaty, the United States representatives signed the Protocol of Queretaro on May 26, 1848, which read, "Conformably to the law of the United States, legitimate titles to every description of property, personal and real, existing in the ceded territories are those which were legitimate titles under the Mexican law in California and New Mexico up to the 13th of May, 1846, and in Texas up to the 2nd of March, 1836.

17. William Henry Ellison, "The United States Indian Policy in California: 1846-1860," 128-139; C. S. Goodrich, "The Legal Status of the California Indians," *California Law Review,* 14 (1926), 7-9.

18. William Carey Jones, Adam Johnston, and Thomas Butler were all such investigators. William Henry Ellison, "The United States Indian Policy in California: 1846-1860," 117, 148-152; William Henry Ellison, "The Federal Indian Policy in California, 1846-1860," *Mississippi Valley Historical Review,* 9 (1922), 42; Record Group 75, Letters Received, Roll 32.

19. Joseph Ellison, *California and the Nation 1850-1869: A Study of the Relations of a Frontier Community with the Federal Government,* 28.

20. Under an enabling act dated September 30, 1850, President Fillmore appointed Redick McKee, George Barbour, and O. M. Wozencraft as commissioners. Record Group 75, Letters Received, Roll 32, pp. 46-47.

21. William Henry Ellison, "The Federal Indian Policy in California, 1846-1860," *Mississippi Valley Historical Review,* 9 (1922), 49-57; Robert W. Kenny, Attorney General of California, *History of the Proposed Settlement of Claims of California Indians.* A number of other publications contain copies of treaties. See Record Group 75, Letters Received, Roll 32.

22. Gregory Crampton, ed., *The Mariposa Indian War 1850-1851: Diaries of Robert Eccleston: The California Gold Rush, Yosemite, and the High Sierra;* William Henry Ellison, "The Federal Indian Policy in California, 1846-1860," *Mississippi Valley Historical Review,* 9 (1922), 49-57; Robert W. Kenny, Attorney General of California, *History of the Proposed Settlement of Claims of California Indians.*

23. William Henry Ellison, "The Federal Indian Policy in California, 1846-1860," *Mississippi Valley Historical Review,* 9 (1922), 58; C. S. Goodrich, "The Legal Status of California Indians," *California Law Review,* 14 (1926), 13-16; Robert W. Kenny, Attorney General of California, *History of the Proposed Settlement of Claims of California Indians.* For a summary of California's

fight to kill the 18 treaties, see Record Group 75, Letters Received, Roll 32, and especially a reprinted article from the *Alta California,* February 24, 1852, p. 0796.

24. Charles Francis Seymour, "Relations Between the United States Government and the Mission Indians of Southern California," 27-37.

25. *Ibid.,* 29.

26. *Ibid.,* 37.

Chapter III

1. The history of the Byrnes case was gleaned from a number of sources: Reports of the Commissioners of Indian Affairs to the Secretary of the Interior; C. C. Painter, *A Visit to the Mission Indians of California and Other Western Tribes;* C. C. Painter, *A Visit to the Mission Indians of California;* C. C. Painter, *The Condition of Affairs in Indian Territories and California. A Report by Prof. C. C. Painter, Agent of the Indian Rights Association;* Papers of the Indian Rights Association; Kate Foote, *The Mission Indians Taxed and Untaxed;* House Report 3251, December 6, 1890, to accompany S. 2783; Senate Executive Document 28, January 13, 1887; House Executive Document 97, January 19, 1892; Helen Hunt Jackson, Report on the Condition and Needs of the Mission Indians; Charles Francis Seymour, "Relations Between the United States Government and the Mission Indians of Southern California; Imre Sutton, "Land Tenure and Changing Occupations on Indian Reservations in Southern California."

2. See Reports of the Commissioners of Indian Affairs.

3. C. C. Painter, *A Visit to the Mission Indians of California,* 13.

4. *San Jacinto Register,* 1930-1935.

5. Report contained in Senate Report 91-1387, December 2, 1970, to accompany H.R. 3328, p. 6.

6. Anthony Madrigal, "Soboba Reservation Water Crisis and Public Law 91-557," an unpublished paper on file with the Soboba band.

7. House Report no. 91-1017, April 23, 1970, to accompany H.R. 3328, p. 6.

8. Report contained in Senate Report 91-1387, December 2, 1970, to accompany H.R. 3328, p. 6.

9. *Ibid.*

10. House Report no. 91-1017, April 23, 1970, to accompany H.R. 3328, p. 6.

11. The events from 1955 through 1958 are contained in Senate Report 91-1387, December 2, 1970, to accompany H.R. 3328.

12. Anthony Madrigal article.

13. *Ibid.*

14. House Report no. 91-1017, April 23, 1970, to accompany H.R. 3328, p. 5.

15. *Ibid.*

16. House Report no. 19-1017, April 23, 1970, to accompany H.R. 3328, p. 11, Senate Report 91-1387, December 2, 1970, to accompany H.R. 3328, p. 7.

17. *Congressional Record,* May 18, 1970, p. 15829.

18. *Ibid.*

19. *Congressional Record,* May 18, 1970, p. 15831-15832.

20. *Hemet News* article, July 29, 1975; *Riverside Press Enterprise* article.

21. Transcript of the meeting taken from a tape made by the author.

22. Transcript of the meeting; *Hemet News* article, September 14, 1974.

23. *Hemet News* articles, June 29, 1977, July 8, 1977, July 9, 1977, July 14, 1977, July 16, 1977, July 20, 1977, August 18, 1977, September 28, 1977, *Riverside Press Enterprise* articles, June 30, 1977, July 12, 1977, July 14, 1977, July 16, 1977, July 20, 1977, July 29, 1977, September 28, 1977.

Chapter IV

1. William Henry Ellison, "Federal Indian Policy in California, 1846-1869," *Mississippi Valley Historical Review,* 9 (1922), 59-60; Record Group 75, Letters Received, Roll 33, p. 0020-0024, 0234-0236.

2. Record Group 75, Letters Received, Roll 33, p. 0023-0024.

3. Record Group 75, Letters Received, Roll 33, p. 0024.

4. William Henry Ellison, "Federal Indian Policy in California, 1846-1869," *Mississippi Valley Historical Review,* 9 (1922), 61-63; Record Group 75, Letters Received, Roll 33, p. 0360-0363, and Roll 34, p. 0177.

5. Letter from the *Daily Morning Call,* February 19, 1858, reproduced in Record Group 75, Roll 36, p. 0667-0668.

6. Record Group 75, Letters Received, Roll 33, p. 0261.

7. William Henry Ellison, "Federal Indian Policy in California, 1846-1869," *Mississippi Valley Historical Review,* 9 (1922), 64-65; Commissioner of Indian Affairs, Report of the Commissioner of Indian Affairs to the Secretary of the Interior, 1856, p. 16-17; Report of the Commissioner of Indian Affairs, 1857, p. 10; Robert F. Heizer, *The Destruction of California Indians,* 89-91; Record Group 75, Letters Received, Roll 33, p. 0374-0376, Roll 34, p. 0646-0648, 0813, 0898, 1036, Roll 35, various reports and letters, 0124-0480.

8. William Henry Ellison, "United States Indian Policy in California, 1846-1860," 173, 183-190.

9. Robert F. Heizer, *The Destruction of California Indians,* 197; Record Group 75, Letters Received, Roll 34, p. 0202-0209.

10. Robert F. Heizer, *The Destruction of California Indians,* 83; Record Group 75, Letters Received, Roll 35, p. 0112-0113, Letter by Henley dated December 29, 1855.

11. Record Group 75, Letters Received, Roll 34, p. 0442-0443.

12. Record Group 75, Letters Received, Roll 33, p. 0435, Roll 34, p. 0148-0153, 0211-0212, 0218.

13. Record Group 75, Letters Received, Roll 37, p. 0063-0072, 0074-0076, 0295-0297, 0597, 0625-0630, 0665-0675.

14. Record Group 75, Letters Received, Roll 38, p. 0162, an editorial from the *Sacramento Union,* January 20, 1861.

15. Record Group 75, Letters Received, Roll 38, p. 0838-0846.

16. Record Group 75, Letters Received, Roll 36, p. 0027-0066, 0117-0136, 0276-0295, Roll 38, p. 0146-0162, 0763.

17. Record Group 75, Letters Received, Roll 37, p. 0080-0085.

18. Report of the Commissioner of Indian Affairs, 1862, p. 313-317; Record Group 75, Letters Received, Roll 38, p. 0484, 0490-0499, 0511-0516, 0625-0636.

19. Report of the Commissioner of Indian Affairs, 1862, p. 311, 320; Report of the Commissioner of Indian Affairs, 1863, p. 91; Record Group 75, Letters Received, Roll 37, p. 1196, Roll 38, p. 0584, 0633-0641, Roll 39, p. 615-619.

20. Record Group 75, Letters Received, Roll 38, p. 0771.

21. Report of the Commissioner of Indian Affairs, 1862, p. 325-328; Report of the Commissioner of Indian Affairs, 1863, p. 101-104; Report of the Commissioner of Indian Affairs, 1864, p. 13; Record Group 75, Letters

Received, Roll 35, p. 0516, Roll 36, p. 0489-0506, Roll 0695-0697, 1125, 1156, 1161, Roll 41; p. 0284-0289.

22. Record Group 75, Letters Received, Roll 38, p. 0455.

23. See footnote 1, Chapter 1.

24. The information about Hoopa was taken from the Reports of the Commissioners of Indian Affairs, 1864-1890, and; Record Group 75, Letters Received, Roll 39, p. 1131-1179.

25. Record Group 75, Letters Received, Roll 39, p. 0985-0989; Roll 40, p. 0551-0557.

26. Record Group 75, Letters Received, Roll 43, p. 0297.

27. Reports of the Commissioners of Indian Affairs, 1868-1890; Record Group 75, Letters Received, Roll 47, pp. 0482-0484, 0879-0883, 0888-0891, Roll 48, pp. 0107-0110, 0123-0125, 0260, 0270-0271, 0288-0290, 0352, 0417-0418, 0423-0424, 0433, 0442-0445, 0527-0530, 0551-0554, 1149-1153, Roll 49, pp. 0031, 0122-0123, 0278, 0282, 0351, 0467, 0539-0541, 0773-0775, 0802-0804.

28. *Ibid.*

29. *Ibid.*

30. The information about Klamath River was taken from the Reports of the Commissioners of Indian Affairs, 1855-1893. The reservation's final demise came with the act of June 17, 1892, "an act to provide for the disposition and lands known as the Klamath River Reservation."

31. The information about Tule River was taken from the Reports of the Commissioners of Indian Affairs, 1864-1879.

32. The information about Round Valley was taken from the Reports of the Commissioners of Indian Affairs, 1864-1904. In 1903 a bill known as the Bell Bill was introduced to Congress that was designed to divert from the Indians the proceeds of sales of thousands of acres of land.

33. The information and opinion of this agent are contained in the Report of the Commissioner of Indian Affairs, 1870, p. 91-95.

34. Report of the Commissioner of Indian Affairs, 1871, p. 345. In the Report of the Commissioner of Indian Affairs, 1872, there is no more agent in the south.

35. Stuart Dagget, *Chapters on the History of the Southern Pacific Railroad.*

36. Report of the Commissioner of Indian Affairs, 1880, p. XXII, 12; Helen Hunt Jackson, Report on the Condition and Needs of the Mission Indians, pp. 20-22.

37. Mission Indian Commission, House Report 691, March 14, 1892; Report of the Commissioner of Indian Affairs, 1882, pp. 251-259; Charles Francis Seymour, "Relations Between the United States Government and the Mission Indians of Southern California," 66-68.

38. Report of the Commissioner of Indian Affairs, 1880, p. XXIII.

39. Report of the Commissioner of Indian Affairs, 1880, p. 12.

40. The report has been published in a number of different places. The one used here was published by the San Jacinto Museum, San Jacinto, California.

41. Senate Executive Document no. 49, forty-fourth Congress, first session contains the bill presented by Chester A. Arthur on January 14, 1884.

42. Committee on Indian Affairs, House. House Report 2556, May 24, 1886, House Report 3251, December 6, 1890, etc. It was finally approved, January 12, 1891.

43. Some minor surveys were conducted, but agents consistently displayed ignorance about the territory. Reports of the Commissioners of Indian Affairs, 1884-1905.

44. Reports of the Commissioners of Indian Affairs, 1895-1905; Jesse Garcia and Philip Webster, *Location and Character of Lands in California*.

45. In case after case, the government neglected to obtain attorneys. In some cases attorneys were only obtained with the financial backing of private citizens. Even when the government did retain attorneys, they often did not get paid or were paid so little that they did not feel inclined to give much attention to cases. Reports of the Commissioners of Indian Affairs, 1883-1905; Charles Francis Seymour, "Relations Between the United States Government and the Mission Indians of Southern California," 73-74; Senate Executive Document 28, January 13, 1887; House Report 3251, December 6, 1890; House Executive Document 97, January 19, 1892; Various Reports of the Special Attorney for the Mission Indians.

46. The removal or non-removal of whites is a constant theme in California and especially among the Mission Indians. Report of the Commissioners of Indian Affairs, 1886-1905.

47. Soboba was an exception because of the Indian Rights Association of Philadelphia. Papers of the Indian Rights Association; Reports of the Commissioners of Indian Affairs, 1888-1901; Charles Francis Seymour, "Relations Between the United States Government and the Mission Indians of Southern California," 42-49; Frank D. Lewis, the government's attorney until 1899 wrote, "The Warner Ranch Indians and Why They were Removed to Pala," *Overland Monthly,* 42 (1903), 171-173.

48. Reports of the Commissioners of Indian Affairs, 1883-1905.

183

49. Reports of the Commissioners of Indian Affairs, 1883-1905.

50. For the land acquisitions between 1893 and 1920, see the Reports of the Commissioners for the same dates. To understand the amount of pressure that had to be applied to the government before it would respond with aid, examine the case of the acquisition of the Pala reservation in Charles Francis Seymour, "Relations Between the United States Government and the Mission Indians of Southern California," 47-49.

51. Reports of the Commissioners of Indian Affairs, 1893-1920, pp. 86-87; Records of Fort Bidwell, Box 22 and 23 in the Federal Archives and Records Center, San Bruno.

52. For Collier's views of the Bureau, The Indian New Deal and the Reorganization Act see John Collier, *Indians of the Americas* and John Collier, *From Every Zenith*. For a more accurate picture of Collier see Lawrence C. Kelly, "The Indian Reorganization Act: The Dream and the Reality," *Pacific Historical Review*, 44 (August, 1975), 291-312.

53. Jesse Garcia and Philip Webster, *Location and Character of Indian Lands in California*.

Chapter V

1. Reports of the Commissioners of Indian Affairs to the Secretary of the Interior.

2. Reports of the Commissioners of Indian Affairs to the Secretary of the Interior. For a biased but useful book dealing with the history of Palm Springs, see Katherine Ainsworth, *The McCallum Saga: The Story of the Founding of Palm Springs*.

3. Senate Report 1522, February 27, 1885, on "Conditions and Needs of Indians of California."

4. Hearings before the Committee on Indian Affairs, House of Representatives, seventy-fifth Congress, third session on H.R. 7450, March 15, 17, 23, 30, April 6, 13, 20, 25, 27, 28, 29, May 4, 11, 18, June 1, 1938, p. 500. Also see those letters dealing with the Agua Caliente reservation contained in the Pearl Chase collection at the University of California, Santa Barbara.

5. 39 STAT. L. 976.

6. Hearings Before the Committee on Indian Affairs, House of Representatives, seventy-fifth Congress, third session on H.R. 7450, March 15, 17, 23, 30, April 6, 13, 20, 25, 27, 28, 29, May 4, 11, 18, June 1, 1938, p. 194; *Los Angeles Times* articles, December 24, 1922, April 29, 1923; *San Francisco Chronicle* article, November 5, 1922; *Los Angeles Examiner* article, February 8,

1923; *Riverside Press* article, February 12, 1923; *Riverside Enterprise* article, February 13, 1923.

7. For discussions of the 1923 allotments see the numerous mentions in Hearings Before the Committee on Indian Affairs, House of Representatives, seventy-fifth Congress, third session on H.R. 7450, March 15, 17, 23, 30, April 6, 13, 20, 25, 27, 28, 29, May 4, 11, 18, June 1, 1938; Hearings Before the Committee on Indian Affairs, House of Representatives, seventy-fifth Congress, first session on H.R. 5297, April 7, 14, and 21, 1937; Hearings Before the Committee on Indian Affairs, United States Senate, seventy-fifth Congress, first session on S. 1424 and S. 2589, October 24, 1935, April 6, 1936, July 6, 24, and August 16, 1937; Hearings Before the Subcommittee on Indian Affairs of the Committee on Public Lands, Hoise of Representatives, eighty-first Congress, first session on H.R. 4616 and H.R. 5310, May 23, 31, June 1, 2, 3, 23, and 27, 1949; Hearings Before House Special Subcommittee on the Committee of Interior and Insular Affairs on Land Allotments on Agua Caliente Reservation, California, October 2, 1957; Hearings Before the Subcommittee on Indian Affairs, House of Representatives, ninetieth Congress, second session on H.R. 17273, May 31, 1968; House Report 86-903 to accompany H.R. 8587, August 14, 1959; *San Diego Tribune* article, November 13, 1923; *Los Angeles Examiner* article, May 1, 1923; *Los Angeles Times* article, May 1, 1923; C. Hart Merriam Collection, carton 14.

8. For a picture of the daily struggle at the Agua Caliente Reservation, see numerous letters contained in the Indian section of the Pearl Chase Collection, University of California, Santa Barbara. The American Indian Defense Association was largely financed from donations sent from the wealthy Santa Barbara chapter. As a result, the national chapter and numerous Indians in need were extremely solicitous of them and sent volumes of letters with information found nowhere else. The same sort of information can be found in the C. Hart Merriam Collection, carton 14.

9. Letters from John Collier to Roy B. Nash, Janury 11, 1923; Letter from the Manager, Agricultural Department of the Los Angeles Chamber of Commerce, October 22, 1923, in the Pearl Chase collection; *Los Angeles Express* article, January 28, 1924.

10. Letters from Lee Arenas to Mr. S. L. Hoffman, May 30, 1924, in the Pearl Chase Collection.

11. The details of the 1927 allotments are discussed throughout the sources listed in fn. 7.

12. Hearings Before the Committee on Indian Affairs, House of Representatives, seventy-fifth Congress, first session on H.R. 5297, April 7, 14, 21, 1937, p. 50.

13. *Ibid*, pp. 87-89.

14. Throughout the sources contained in fn. 7, once can find the testimony from both sides.

15. Hearings Before the Committee on Indian Affairs, House of Representatives, seventy-fifth Congress, first session on H.R. 5207, April 7, 14, 21, 1937, pp.1-3; Hearings Before the Committee on Indian Affairs, House of Representatives, seventy-fifth Congress, third session on H.R. 7450, March 15, 17, 23, 30, April 6, 13, 20, 25, 27, 28, 29, May 4, 11, 118, June 1, 1938, p. 39.

16. H.R. 8600 and S. 3268; Hearings in Hearings Before the Committee on Indian Affairs, United States Senate, seventy-fifth Congress, first session on S. 1424 and S. 2589, October 24, 1935, April 16, 1936, July 6, 29, August 16, 1937; Hearings Before the Committee on Indian Affairs, House of Representatives, seventy-fifth Congress, first session on H.R. 5297, April 7, 14, 21, 1937, p. 58; House Report 74-1521, July 15, 1935, to accompany H.R. 8600; *Palm Springs Desert Sun* article, December 20, 1935; *Riverside Enterprise* article, December 29, 1935.

17. Hearings Before the Committee on Indian Affairs, House of Representatives, seventy-fifth Congress, first session on H.R. 5297, April 7, 14, 21, 1937, pp. 73, 87-89; Hearings Before the Committee on Indian Affairs, United States Senate, seventy-fifth Congress, first session on S. 1424 and S. 2589, October 24, 1935, April 16, 1936, July 6, 29, August 16, 1937, pp. 55, 184-186, 199-266; Hearings Before the Committee on Indian Affairs, House of Representatives, seventy-fifth Congress, third session on H.R. 7450, March 15, 17, 23, 30, April 6, 13, 20, 25, 27, 28, 29, May 4, 11, 18, June 1, 1938, pp. 45, 66-68, 192, 490.

18. Hearings Before the Committee on Indian Affairs, House of Representatives, seventy-fifth Congress, third session on H.R. 7450, March 15, 17, 23, 30, April 6, 13, 20, 25, 27, 28, 29, May 4, 11, 18, June 1, 1938, p. 518.

19. Hearings Before the Committee on Indian Affairs, House of Representatives, seventy-fifth Congress, first session on H.R. 5297, April 7, 14, 21, 1937, p. 173.

20. Hearings Before the Committee on Indian Affairs, United States Senate, seventy-fifth Congress, first session on S. 1424 and S. 2589, October 24, 1935, April 16, 1936, July 6, 29, August 16, 1937, pp. 184-186. Also see the sources in fn. 17.

21. Hearings Before the Committee on Indian Affairs, House of Representatives, seventy-fifth Congress, first session on H.R. 5297, April 7, 14, 21, 1937, p. 55; Hearings Before the Committee on Indian Affairs, House of Representatives, seventh-fifth Congress, third session on H.R. 7450, March 15, 17, 23, 30, April 6, 13,20, 25, 27, 28, 29, May 4, 11, 18, June 1, 1938, p. 490; *Los Angeles Times* article, November 7, 1936; *Palm Springs Desert*

Sun, November 6, 1936; *Palm Springs Limelight,* November 7, 1936.

22. Hearings Before the Committee on Indian Affairs, House of Representatives, seventh-fifth Congress, third session on H.R. 7450, March 15, 17, 23, 30, April 6, 13, 20, 25, 27, 28, 29, May 4, 11, 18, June 1, 1938, p. 491; Records of the Palm Springs Agency, Correspondence, 1938-1950; Box 2, folder marked "operating instructions" contains the letter from John Collier to Mr. John Dady, November 6, 1937, outlining the Palm Springs course of action. Federal Records Center, Laguna Nigel.

23. Hearings Before the Committee on Indian Affairs, House of Representatives, seventy-fifth Congress, third session on H.R. 7450, March 15, 17, 23, 30, April 6, 13, 20, 25, 27, 28, 29, May 4, 11, 18, June 1, 1938, pp. 149, 268-362, 385-402, 491; *Los Angeles Examiner* articles, January 5 and 7, 1937; *Los Angeles Times* article, November 7, 1936; *Palm Springs News* article, January 7, 1937.

24. H.R. 5297 and S. 1424.

25. H.R. 2589 and H.R. 7450.

26. Hearings Before the Committee on Indian Affairs, House of Representatives, seventy-fifth Congress, first session on H.R. 5297, April 7, 14, 21, 1937, pp. 26-29.

27. Hearings Before the Committee on Indian Affairs, House of Representatives, seventy-fifth Congress, third session on H.R. 7450, March 15, 17, 23, 30, April 6, 13, 20, 25, 27, 28, 29, May 4, 11, 18, June 1, 1938, pp. 14-16.

28. Hearings Before the Committee on Indian Affairs, United States Senate, seventy-fifth Congress, first session on S. 1424 and S. 2589, October 24, 1935, April 16, 1936, July 6, 29, August 16, 1937, pp. 100-101; Report from Acting Secretary of the Interior Charles West to the President of the Senate, May 28, 1937.

29. Hearings Before the Committee on Indian Affairs, United States Senate, seventy-fifth Congress, first session on S. 1424 and S. 2589, October 24, 1935, April 16, 1936, July 6, 29, August 16, 1937, pp. 165, 258-266.

30. Hearings Before the Committee on Indian Affairs, House of Representatives, seventy-fifth Congress, third session on H.R. 7450, March 15, 17, 23, 30, April 6, 13, 20, 25, 27, 28, 29, May 4, 11, 18, June 1, 1938, pp. 64-65, 326, 374, 478-479, 492-493.

31. Hearings Before the Committee on Indian Affairs, United States Senate, seventy-fifth Congress, first session on S. 1424 and S. 2589, October 24, 1935, April 16, 1936, July 6, 29, August 16, 1937, pp. 256-258;

Hearings Before the Committee on Indian Affairs, House of Representatives, seventy-fifth Congress, third session on H.R. 7450, March 15, 17, 23, 30, April 6, 13, 20, 25, 27, 28, 29, May 4, 11, 18, June 1, 1938, pp. 25-26, 54, 68, 268-362.

32. Hearings Before the Committee on Indian Affairs, House of Representatives, seventy-fifth Congress, third session on H.R. 7450, March 15, 17, 23, 30, April 6, 13, 20, 25, 27, 28, 29, May 4, 11, 18, June 1, 1938, p. 303.

33. Hearings Before the Committee on Indian Affairs, House of Representatives, seventy-fifth Congress, third session on H.R. 7450, March 15, 17, 23, 30, April 6, 13, 20, 25, 27, 28, 29, May 4, 11, 18, June 1, 1938, pp. 275-278, 318-330, 372-373.

34. Hearings Before the Committee on Indian Affairs, House of Representatives, seventy-fifth Congress, third session on sH.R. 7450, March 15, 17, 23, 30, April 6, 13, 20, 25, 27, 28, 29, May 4, 11, 18, June 1, 1938, pp. 25-26, 282, 373-378.

35. Hearings Before the Committee on Indian Affairs, House of Representatives, seventy-fifth Congress, third session on H.R. 7450, March 15, 17, 23, 20, April 6, 13, 20, 25, 27, 28, 28, May 4, 11, 18, June 1, 1938, pp. 86, 373-374; Records of the Riverside Area Field Office, Federal Records Center, Laguna Nigel, Box 11, "Tibbet Case."

36. Hearings Before the Committee on Indian Affairs, House of Representatives, seventy-fifth Congress, third session on H.R. 7450, March 15, 17, 23, 30, April 6, 13, 20, 25, 27, 28, 29, May 4, 11, 18, June 1, 1938, pp. 25-26, 362-383.

37. Hearings Before the Committee on Indian Affairs, House of Representatives, seventy-fifth Congress, third session on H.R. 7450, March 15, 17, 23, 30, April 6, 13, 20, 25, 27, 28, 29, May 4, 11, 18, June 1, 1938, pp. 37-41, 134-135, 143.

38. Hearings Before a Special Subcommittee of the Committee on Interior and Insular Affairs, House of Representatives, eighty-fifth Congress, first session, on Equalization of Land Allotments on Agua Caliente Reservation, California, October 2, 1957, pp. 4, 82-83; 24 F. Supp. 237; 158 F. 2nd 730; 322 U.S. 419; 137 F. 2nd 199; 108 F. 2nd 876.

39. Hearings Before a Special Subcommittee of the Committee on Interior and Insular Affairs, House of Representatives, eighty-fifth Congress, first session on Equalization of Land Allotments on Agua Caliente Reservation, California, October 2, 1957, pp. 83, 86.

40. Hearings Before a Special Subcommittee of the Committee on Interior and Insular Affairs, House of Representatives, eighty-fifth Congress,

first session on Equalization of Land Allotments on Agua Caliente Reservation, California, October 2, 1957, pp. 4, 88, 101-105.

41. For a discussion of the activities of John Leytel, see Hearings Before a Special Subcommittee of the Committee on Interior and Insular Affairs, House of Representatives, eighty-fifth Congress, first session on Equalization of Land Allotments on Agua Caliente Reservation, California, October 2, 1957, pp. 85, 88.

42. Hearings Before a Special Subcommittee of the Committee on Interior and Insular Affairs, House of Representatives, eighty-fifth Congress, first session on Equalization of Land Allotments on Agua Caliente Reservation, California, October 2, 1957, p. 83; Hearings Before the Subcommittee on Indian Affairs of the Committee on Public Lands, House of Representatives, eighty-first Congress, first session on H.R. 4616 and H.R. 5310, May 23, 31, June 1, 2, 3, 23, and 27, 1949, pp. 29-87.

43. Hearings Before a Special Subcommittee of the Committee on Interior and Insular Affairs, House of Representatives, eighty-fifth Congress, first session on Equalization of Land Allotments on Agua Caliente Reservation, California, October 2, 1957, pp. 84, 88.

44. Hearings Before a Special Subcommittee of the Committee on Interior and Insular Affairs, House of Representatives, eighty-fifth Congress, first session on Equalization of Land Allotments on Agua Caliente Reservation, California, October 2, 1957, 88-89; Hearings Before the Subcommittee on Indian Affairs of the Committee on Public Lands, House of Representatives, eight-first Congress, first session on H.R. 4616 and H.R. 5310, May 23, 31, June 1, 2, 3, and 27, 1949, pp. 83-84.

45. For a discussion of the Segundo and Pierce cases, see Hearings Before a Special Subcommittee of the Committee on Interior and Insular Affairs, House of Representatives, eighty-fifth Congress, first session on Equalization of Land Allotments on Agua Caliente Reservation, California, October 2, 1957, pp. 5, 74-116; 123 F. Supp. 554; 235 F. 2nd 885.

46. Hearings Before the Subcommittee on Indian Affairs of the Committee on Public Lands, House of Representatives, eighty-first Congress, first session on H.R. 4616 and H. R. 5310, May 23, 31, June 1, 2, 3, 23, and 27, 1949; Hearings Before a Special Subcommittee of the Committee on Interior and Insular Affairs, House of Representatives, eighty-fifth Congress, first session on Equalization of Land Allotments on Agua Caliente Reservation, California, October 2, 1957, pp. 92-93.

47. Hearings Before a Special Subcoomittee of the Committee on Interior and Insular Affairs, House of Representatives, eighty-fifth Congress, first session on Equalization of Land Allotments on Agua Caliente Reservation, California, October 2, 1957, pp. 5, 74-116; 123 F. Supp. 554; 235 F. 2nd 885.

48. *Program For the Termination of Indian Activities in the State of California.* Prepared by the California Indian Agency, Sacramento, California, submitted by the Commissioner of Indian Affairs, June, 1949, by Walter V. Woehlke, State Director; Hearings Before a Special Subcommittee of the Committee on Interior and Insular Affairs, House of Representatives, eighty-fifth Congress, first session on Equalization of Land Allotments on Agua Caliente Reservation, California, October 2, 1957, pp. 94-95.

49. Hearings Before a Special Subcommittee of the Committee on Interior and Insular Affairs, House of Representatives, eighty-fifth Congress, first session on Equalization of Land Allotments on Agua Caliente Reservation, California, October 2, 1957.

50. House Report 86-903 to accompany H.R. 8587, August 14, 1959; United States Department of Interior Report on the Administration of Guardianship and Conservatorships Established for Members of the Agua Caliente Band of Mission Indians, California, March 1968, contained in Hearings Before the Subcommittee on Indian Affairs of the Committee on Interior and Insular Affairs, House of Representatives, ninetieth Congress, second session on H.R. 17273, May 31, 1968, p. 30.

51. For the Bureau ruling, see 25 CFR 124.5; Hearings Before the Subcommittee on Indian Affairs of the Committee on Interior and Insular Affairs, House of Representatives, ninetieth Congress, second session on H.R. 17273, May 31, 1968, pp. 30-32, 85-86, 110.

52. Hearings Before the Subcommittee on Indian Affairs of the Committee on Interior and Insular Affairs, House of Representatives, ninetieth Congress, second session on H.R. 17273, May 31, 1968, p. 32.

53. Hearings Before the Subcommittee on Indian Affairs of the Committee on Interior and Insular Affairs, House of Representatives, ninetieth Congress, second session on H.R. 17273, May 31, 1968, pp. 130, 160.

54. Public Law 86-327, September 21, 1959.

55. Hearings Before the Subcommittee on Indian Affairs of the Committee on Interior and Insular Affairs, House of Representatives, ninetieth Congress, second session on H.R. 17273, May 31, 1968, pp. 33, 102-107.

56. For letters exchanged between Dawson, Udall, and Carver, see exhibits of the Reports in Hearings Before the Subcommittee on Indian Affairs of the Committee on Interior and Insular Affairs, House of Representatives, ninetieth Congress, second session on H.R. 17273, May 31, 1968, pp. 87-92.

57. Hearings Before the Subcommittee on Indian Affairs of the Commit-

tee on Interior and Insular Affairs, House of Representatives, ninetieth Congress, second session on H.R. 17273, May 31, 1968, p. 33.

58. Hearings Before the Subcommittee on Indian Affairs of the Committee on Interior and Insular Affairs, House of Representatives, ninetieth Congress, second session on H.R. 17273, May 31, 1968, pp. 34, 50-53.

59. Letter of Charles Renda, Regional Solicitor, Sacramento Region, May 12, 1967, in Hearings Before the Subcommittee on Indian Affairs of the Committee on Interior and Insular Affairs, House of Representatives, ninetieth Congress, second session on H.R. 17273, May 31, 1968, p. 93. For a summary of the report and the hearing, see *Los Angeles Times* articles, April 3 and June 1, 1968.

60. Hearings Before the Subcommittee on Indian Affairs of the Committee on Interior and Insular Affairs, House of Representatives, ninetieth Congress, second session on H.R. 17273, May 31, 1968, pp. 96-97.

61. Hearings Before the Subcommittee on Indian Affairs of the Committee on Interior and Insular Affairs, House of Representatives, ninetieth Congress, second session on H.R. 17273, May 31, 1968, pp. 96-97. Two adults retained conservators at their own request and a number of minors retained their guardians at the request of their parents.

62. *Los Angeles Times* articles July 18 and 27, 1977; *Riverside Press Enterprise* article, April 1, 1976.

63. Report of the City Manager of Palm Springs, May, 1966, p. 5; *Los Angeles Times* articles, July 18 and 27, 1977; *Riverside Press Enterprise* article, April 1, 1976.

64. *Los Angeles Times* articles, May 19, 1972, and July 18, 1977.

65. *Los Angeles Times* article, July 18, 1977.

66. *Riverside Press Enterprise* article, April 1, 1976.

67. *Los Angeles Times* articles, June 21, July 18 and July 27, 1977.

68. *Los Angeles Times* articles, July 18 and July 27, 1977.

69. *Los Angeles Times* articles, July 27, 1977.

Chapter VI

1. March 3, 1863, (12 STAT 765-767); Senate Report No. 778, eightieth Congress, first session on the Indian Claims Commission, December 12, 1947, p. 3; H.R. 12788, sixty-sixth Congress, second session.

2. Hearings Before the Committee on Indian Affairs, United States Senate, seventy-seventh Congress, first session on S 710, S 1112, and S 1366,

191

June 17 and 18, 1941, memorandum of information; Relief of Certain Mission Indians in California, Senate Report No. 469, fifty-seventh Congress, first session, February 14, 1902; Draft of a Bill for the Relief of Certain Indians of California, January 27, 1902.

3. Robert W. Kenny, Attorney General of California, *History of the Proposed Settlement: Claims of California Indians,* 25-26; Kenneth M. Johnson, *K-3444 or the California Indians vs the United States.*

4. Hearings Before the Committee on Indian Affairs, United States Senate, seventy-fourth Congress, first session on S 1793, part 2, July 25, 1935, p. 148.

5. Hearings Before the Committee on Indian Affairs, United States House of Representatives, seventy-sixth Congress, first session on H.R. 3765, March 25, 29, 31, 1939, and hearings before the subcommittee April 6, 7, 13, 14, 17, 19, 20, 21, 24, 1939, p. 13.

6. C. E. Kelsey, *Report of the Special Agent for California Indians to the Commissioner of Indian Affairs;* Department of Interior Report 1906 cited in Hearings before the Committee on Indian Affairs, United States House of Representatives, seventy-sixth Congress, first session on H.R. 3765, March 25, 29, 31, 1939, and hearings before the subcommittee April 6, 7, 13, 14, 17, 19, 20, 21, 24, 1939, p. 17; Mr. Malcolm McDowell Survey contained in the fifty-first Annual Report of the Board of Indian Commissioners to the Secretary of the Interior for the fiscal year ended June 30, 1920, and it is summarized in John G. Rockwell, *The Status of the Indians in California Today.*

7. Hearings Before the Committee on Indian Affairs, United States House of Representatives, seventy-sixth Congress, first session on H.R. 3765, March 25, 29, 31, 1939, and hearings before the subcommittee April 6, 7, 13, 14, 17, 19, 20, 21, 24, 1939, p. 10.

8. Hearings Before the Committee on Indian Affairs, United States Senate, seventy-seventh Congress, first session on S 710, S 1112, and S 1366, June 17 and 18, 1941, p. 6; Hearings Before the Committee on Indian Affairs, United States Senate, seventy-fourth Congress, first session on S 1793, Part 2, July 25, 1935; Hearings Before a Subcommittee of the Committee of Indian Affairs of the House of Representatives on H.R. 8036 and H.R. 9497, May 5, 1926.

9. Hearings Before a Subcommittee of the Committee on Indian Affairs of the House of Representatives on H.R. 8036 and H.R. 9497, May 5, 1926.

10. (STATS 1927, p. 1092) "An Act to authorize the attorney general to bring suit in he Court of Claims in behalf of the Indians of the State of California in the event that the Congress of the United States authorizes the same; Robert W. Kenny, Attorney General of California, *History of the Proposed Settlement; Claims of California Indians,* p. 27.

192

11. Jurisdictional Act of 1928 (Amended by an Act of April 29, 1930) H.R. 491, "An Act to authorize the attorney general of the State of California to bring suit in the Court of Claims on behalf of the Indians of California. When the case entered the Court of Claims it came to be known as K-344.

12. Hearings Before the Committee on Indian Affairs, House of Representatives, seventieth Congress, first session on H.R. 491, March 8 and 15, 1928, and before a subcommittee, February 29, 1928.

13. Jurisdictional Act of 1928; Hearings Before the Committee on Indian Affairs, United States Senate, seventy-seventh Congress, first session on S 710, S 1112, and S 1366, June 17 and 18, 1941.

14. Reid Peyton Chambers, "A Study of Administrative Conflict of Interest in the Protection of Indian Natural Resources," published in Hearings Before the Subcommittee on Administrative Practices and Procedures of the Committee on the Judiciary, United States Senate, ninety-second Congress, first session on Adminitsrative Practices and Procedures Relating to Protection of Indian Natural Resources, Part L, October 19 and 20, 1971, pp. 233-249.

15. Hearings Before the Committee on Indian Affairs, United States Senate, seventy-fourth Congress, first session on S 1793, Part 2, July 25, 1935, p. 130, 134-137; Survey of Conditions of Indians in United States, Hearings Before Senate Subcommittee, seventy-second Congress, first session, September 28-29, 1932; Survey of Conditions of Indians in United States, Hearings Before Senate Subcommittee, seventy-third Congress, June 29 to July 2, 1934.

16. Hearings Before the Committee on Indian Affairs, United States Senate, seventy-seventh Congress, first session on S 710, S 1112, and S 1366, June 17 and 18, 1941, pp. 91, 100-106.

17. Hearings Before the Committee on Indian Affairs, United States Senate, seventy-fourth Congress, first session on S 1793, Part 2, July 25, 1935; Survey of Conditions of Indians in United States Hearings Before the Senate, seventy-third Congress, June 29 and July 2, 1934; Hearings Before the Committee on Indian Affairs, United States Senate, seventy-fifth Congress, first session on S 1641, March 8, 9, 11, and 12, 1937; Hearings Before the Committee on Indian Affairs, House of Representatives, seventy-fifth Congress, first session on S 1641, August 10, 12, 13, 1937; Hearings Before the Committee on Indian Affairs, House of Representatives, seventy-sixth Congress, first session on H.R. 3765, March 25-31, and Hearings Before Subcommittee, April 6, 7, 10, 13, 14, 17, 19, 20, 21, 24, 1939; Hearings Before the Committee on Indian Affairs, United States Senate, seventy-seventh Congress, first session on S 710, S 1112, and S 1366, June 17 and 18, 1941.

18. *Ibid.*

19. Hearing Before the Committee on Indian Affairs, United States Senate, seventy-fourth Congress, first session on S 1793, Part 2, July 25, 1935, pp. 140-142.

20. Survey of Conditions of Indians in the United States, Hearings Before a Subcommittee of the Committee on Indian Affairs, United States Senate, seventieth Congress, second session, Part 2, November 19, 20, 22, 23, and 26, 1928, pp. 751-752; Hearings Before the Committee on Indian Affairs, United States Senate, seventy-fourth Congress, first session on S 1793, Part 2, July 25, 1935, pp. 99-140; Hearings Before the Committee on Indian Affairs, House of Representatives, seventy-fifth Congress, third session on H.R. 7450, March 15, 17, 23, 30, April 6, 13, 20, 25, 27, 28, 29, May 4, 11, 18, and June 1, 1938; Hearings Before the Subcommittee on Indian Affairs of the Committee on Public Lands, House of Representatives, eighty-first Congress, first session on H.R. 4616 and H.R. 5310, May 23, 31, June 1, 2, 3, 23, and 27, 1949, pp. 83-84; Hearings Before the Committee on Indian Affairs, United States Senate, eighty-eighth Congress, first session, May 24, 1963; pp. 24-25; *American Indian Life*, 4 (November-December, 1934) 11; C. Hart Merriam Collection, Bancroft Library, Carton 14; Mission Indian Records, Federal Records Center, Laguna Nigel, Box 58471.

21. The infighting is evident in many of the documents. If one wants to see how vicious it could get, see the various issues of *California Indian News*. Also see the various papers in the Pearl Chase Collection; C. Hart Merriam Collection, Bancroft Library, Carton 14; Papers of the California League for American Indians, Bancroft Library, Carton 11; Mission Indian Records, Federal Records Center, Laguna Nigel, Box 33237.

22. Hearings Before the Committee on Indian Affairs, House of Representatives, seventy-sixth Congress, first session on H.R. 3765, March 25-31, and Hearings Before the Subcommittee, April 6, 7, 10, 13, 14, 17, 19, 20, 21, 24, 1939; S 1793, seventy-fourth Congress, first session, 1939; H.R. 3765, seventy-sixth Congress, first session, 1939; S 710, seventy-seventh Congress, first session, 1941; H.R. 5704, seventy-seventh Congress, first session, 1941; S 1651, seventy-fifth Congress, first session, 1937; H.R. 1998, seventy-fifth Congress, first session, 1937; S 1112, seventy-seventh Congress, first session, 1941; H.R. 6474, seventy-seventh Congress, second session, 1942; H.R. 3168, seventy-eighth Congress, first session, 1943; H.R. 4572, seventy-eighth Congress, second session, 1944; H.R. 5089, seventy-eighth Congress, second session, 1944; Robert W. Kenny, Attorney General of California, *History of the Proposed Settlement; Claims of California Indians*, 36-38.

23. Hearings Before the Committee on Indian Affairs, House of Representatives, seventy-sixth Congress, first session on H.R. 3765, March 25-31, and Hearings Before the Subcommittee, April 6, 7, 10, 13, 14, 17, 19, 20, 21, 24, 1939; Hearings Before the Committee on Indian Affairs, United States

Senate, seventy-seventh Congress, first session on S 710, S 1112, and S 1366, June 17 and 18, 1941; Hearings Before the Committee on Indian Affairs, House of Representatives, seventy-fifth Congress on S 1651, August 10, 12, 13, 1937, p. 6; Hearings Before the Committee on Indian Affairs, United States Senate, seventy-fifth Congress, first session on S 1651, March 8, 9, 11, and 12, 1937, p. 3; President Roosevelt's message at the veto of S 1793; *Congressional Record,* June 30, 1936, p. 10561.

24. Senate Report No. 381, August 12, 1969, compensating the Indians of California for the value of land erroneously used as an offset in a judgment against the United States obtained by said Indians; House Report 334, June 30, 1969, compensating the Indians of California for the value of land erroneously used as an offset in a judgment against the United States by said Indians; H.R. 671 approved August 25, 1969.

25. Mr. Malcolm McDowell survey contained in the fifty-first Annual Report of the Board of Indian Commissioners to the Secretary of the Interior for the fiscal year ended June 30, 1920, and summarized in John G. Rockwell, *The Status of the Indians in California Today.*

26. The 1928 Jurisdictional Act, section 3.

27. Hearings Before the Committee on Indian Affairs, United States Senate, seventy-seventh Congress, first session on S 710, S 1112, and S 1366, June 17 and 18, 1941, p. 52.

28. Hearings Before the Committee on Indian Affairs, House of Representatives, seventy-sixth Congress, first session on H.R. 3765, March 25-31, 1939, and Hearings Before Subcommittee, April 6, 7, 10, 13, 14, 17, 19, 20, 21, 24, 1939, p. 19.

29. Hearings Before the Committee on Indian Affairs, House of Representatives, seventy-fifth Congress, first session on S 1651, August 10, 12, 13, 1937; Hearings Before the Committee on Indian Affairs, United States Senate, seventy-fifth Congress, first session on S 1641, March 8, 9, 11, and 12, 1937.

30. Hearings Before Subcommittee on Indian Affairs, Interior and Insular Affairs Committee, House of Representatives, eighty-ninth Congress, second session on H.R. 8021, May 2 and 3, 1966, pp. 189-190.

31. Robert W. Kenny, Attorney General of California, *History of the Proposed Settlement; Claims of California Indians,* pp. 43-44; Kenneth M. Johnson, *K-344 on the California Indians vs. the United States,* pp. 40-41.

32. Robert W. Kenny, Attorney General of California, *History of the Proposed Settlement; Claims of California Indians,* pp. 44-49.

33. Hearings Before Subcommittee on Indian Affairs Interior and Insular Affairs Committee, House of Representatives, eighty-ninth Congress,

second session on H.R. 8021, May 2 and 3, 1966, p. 207; The case is mentioned in its early stages in Hearings Before the Committee on Indian Affairs, House of Representatives, seventy-sixth Congress, first session on H.R. 3765, March 25-31, and Hearings Before the Subcommittee, April 6, 7, 10, 13, 14, 17, 19, 20, 21, 24, 1939, pp. 17-18.

34. Hearings Before the Subcommittee on Indian Affairs of the Committee on Interior and Insular Affairs, House of Representatives, eighty-eighth Congress, first session, May 24, 1963, pp. 24-25.

35. Public Law 726, seventy-ninth Congress created the Commission, August 13, 1946. The first meeting was in 1947. From Senate Report No. 778, eightieth Congress on Indian Claims Commission, December 12, 1947. For an interesting article on the biased nature of the Indian Claims Commission, see anonymous, "Systematic Discrimination in the Indian Claims Commission: The Burden of Proof in Redressing Historical Wrongs," *Iowa Law Review*, 57, (June, 1972), 1300-1319.

36. Hearings Before the Subcommittee on Indian Affairs on the Committee on Interior and Insular Affairs, House of Representatives, eighty-eighth Congress, first session, May 24, 1963, pp. 27, 31-32, 37-38, 41-43; Hearings Before the Subcommittee on Indian Affairs of the Interior and Insular Affairs Committee, House of Representatives, eighty-ninth Congress, second session on H.R. 8021, May 2 and 3, 1966, p. 197.

37. H.R. 1354 (64 STAT. 189); Senate Report No. 1265, eightieth Congress, second session, May 10, 1948.

38. Hearings Before the Subcommittee on Indian Affairs of the Interior and Insular Affairs Committee, House of Representatives, eighty-eighth Congress, second session on H.R. 8021, May 2 and 3, 1966, p. 3; Senate Report No. 91-381, August 12, 1969, "Compensating the Indians of California for the value of land erroneously used as an offset in a judgment against the United States obtained by said Indians," p. 1; Senate Report No. 90-1513, September 9, 1968, "Providing for Preparations of a Roll of Persons of California Indian Descent and the Distribution of Certain Judgment Funds," p. 5.

39. House Report No. 90-1478, May 27, 1968, "Providing for Preparation of a Roll of Persons of California Indian Descent and the Distribution of Certain Judgment Funds," to accompany H.R. 10911, pp. 7-8; Senate Report 90-1513, September 9, 1968, "Providing for Preparation for a Roll of Persons of California Indian Descent and the Distribution of Certain Judgment Funds," pp. 1-7; Hearings Before the Subcommittee on Indian Affairs, House of Representatives, eighty-eighth Congress, 1963, pp. 37-38.

40. House Report No. 90-1478, May 27, 1968, "Providing for Preparation of a Roll of Persons of California Indian Descent and the Distribution of

Certain Judgment Funds," to accompany H.R. 10911, pp. 7-8; Senate Report No. 90-1513, September 9, 1968, "Providing for Preparation of a Roll of Persons of California Indian Descent and the Distribution of Certain Judgment Funds," pp. 1-7; Hearings Before the Subcommittee on Indian Affairs, Interior and Insular Affairs Committee, House of Representatives, eighty-ninth Congress, second session on H.R. 8021, May 2 and 3, 1966, p. 209.

41. Indian Affairs Bureau, Interior Department, *Indians of California,* 1966; House Report No. 90-1478, May 27, 1968, "Providing for Preparation of a Roll of Persons of California Indian Descent and the Distribution of Certain Judgment Funds," to accompany H.R. 10911, pp. 8-9 give the figure of around 80 million acres for the decision as does House Report 92-974, March 29, 1972, "Amending section 5 of the Act of September 21, 1968," p. 5.

42. House Report No. 90-1478, May 27, 1968, "Providing for Preparation of a Roll of Persons of California Indian Descent and the Distribution of Certain Judgment Funds," to accompany H.R. 10911, pp. 7-8; Senate Report No. 90-1513, September 9, 1968, "Providing for Preparation of a Roll of Persons of California Indian Descent and the Distribution of Certain Judgment Funds," pp. 1-7; Additional Hearings Before the Subcommittee of the Committee on Appropriations, House of Representatives, eighty-first Congress, second session, Additional Hearings, Mission Indians; House Report No. 92-964, March 29, 1972, "Amending Section 5 of the Act of September 21, 1968, pp. 5-6.

43. House Report No. 90-1478, May 27, 1968, "Providing for Preparation of a Roll of Persons of California Indian Descent and the Distribution of Certain Judgment Funds," to accompany H.R. 10911, pp. 7-8; Senate Report No. 90-1513, September 9, 1968, "Providing for Preparation of a Roll of Persons of California Indian Descent and the Distribution of Certain Judgment Funds," p. 9; Hearings Before the Subcommittee on Indian Affairs, Interior and Insular Affairs Committee of the House of Representatives, eighty-ninth Congress, second session on H.R. 8021, May 2 and 3, 1966.

44. House Report No. 90-1478, May 27, 1968, "Providing for Preparation of a Roll of Persons of California Indian Descent and the Distribution of Certain Judgment Funds," to accompany H.R. 10911, pp. 7-8; Hearings Before the Subcommittee on Indian Affairs, Interior and Insular Affairs Committee of the House of Representatives, eighty-ninth Congress, second session on H.R. 8021, May 2 and 3, 1966, pp. 195-216; Senate Report No. 90-1513, September 9, 1968, "Providing for Preparation of a Roll of Persons of California Indian Descent and the Distribution of Certain Judgment Funds," pp. 1-7; Hearings Before the Subcommittee on Indian Affairs, House of Representatives, eighty-eighth Congress, 1963, pp. 37-78.

197

45. See Chapter IV.

46. Robert F. Kennedy, "Buying it Back from the Indians," *Life,* 52, no. 2 (March 23, 1962), 17-19.

47. House Report No. 92-964, March 29, 1972, "Amending Section 5 of the Act of September 21, 1968."

Bibliography

BOOKS AND PERIODICALS

Ainsworth, Katherine, *The McCallum Saga: The Story of the Founding of Palm Springs,* Palm Springs, California, The Palm Springs Desert Museum, 1973.

Allen, Jack and Dennis Moristo, *An Introduction to the Bureau of Indian Affairs. Agency Records and Bureau of Indian Affairs-Archival Records Housed in the San Francisco and Bell Federal Records Centers.* Los Angeles, American Indian Culture Center, Los Angeles, 1971.

Almstedt, Ruth Farrell, *Bibliography of the Diegueno Indians,* Ramona, California, Ballena Press, 1974.

American Friends Service Committee, *Indians of California, Past and Present,* San Francisco, 1956.

The American Indian Federation, *The American Indian.*

American Indian Historical Society, *The Indian Historian,* San Francisco.

Ames, John G., *Report of Special Agent John G. Ames in Regard to Conditions of the Mission Indians of California with Recommendations.* Washington, D.C., Government Printing Office, 1873.

Arnold, M. E. and M. Reed, *In the Land of the Grasshopper Song.* New York, Vantage Press, 1957.

Association of American Indian Affairs, *Indian Affairs,* New York.

—————, *The American Indian,* New York.

Bancroft, Hubert Howe, *History of California,* 3 vols., San Francisco, The History Co., 1890.

—————, *The Native Races of the Pacific States of North America,* 5 vols., San Francisco, A. L. Bancroft & Co., 1882, 1883.

Bannon, John Francis, ed., *Indian Labor in the Spanish Indies,* Lexington, Massachussetts, Toronto, London, D. C. Heath and Co., 1966.

Barrows, David Prescot, *The Ethnobotany of the Coahuilla Indians of Southern California,* Banning, California, Malki Museum Press, 1967.

Baumhoff, M. A., *Econological Determinants of Aboriginal California Population,* Berkeley and Los Angeles, University of California Publications in American Archaeology and Ethnology, Vol. 49, no. 2, pp. 155-236, 1963.

—————, *California Athapascan Groups,* Berkeley, University of California Press, 1958.

Beals, Ralph L. and Joseph A. Hoster, *Indian Occupancy, Subsistence and Land Use Patterns in California.* In the David Agee Horr *American Indian Ethnohistory* series, New York and London, Garland Publishing, Inc., 1974.

Bean, Lowell John, and Thomas F. King, eds., *ANTAP: California Indian Political and Economic Organization,* Ramona, California, Ballena Press, 1974.

—————, and Harry Lawton, *A Bibliography of the Coahuilla Indians of California,* Banning, California, Malki Museum Press, 1967.

—————, and Sylvia Brakke Vane, *California Indians: Primary Resources: A Guide to Manuscripts, Artifacts, Documents, Serials,*

200

Music and Illustrations. Ramona, California, Ballena Press, 1977.

—————, and Harry Lawton, *The Coahuilla Indians of Southern California; Their History and Culture,* Banning, California, Malki Museum Press, 1965.

—————, *Mukat's People: The Coahuilla Indians of Southern California.* Berkeley and Los Angeles, University of California Press, 1972.

—————, and Katherine Siva Saubel, *Temalpakh: Coahuilla Indian Knowledge and Usage of Plants.* Banning, California, Malki Museum Press, 1972.

Beatty, Donald R., *History of the Legal Status of the American Indian with Particular Reference to California.* San Francisco, R and E Research Associates, 1974.

Blanchard, Carol, and Edward E. Hill, *Indian Census Rolls 1885-1940.* Washington, National Archives and Record Service, 1967.

Bleeker, Sonia, *The Mission Indians of California,* New York, William Morrow and Company, Inc., 1956.

Bonsal, Stephen, *Edward Fitzgerald Beal, A Pioneer in the Path of Empire, 1822-1903.* New York and London, G. P. Putnam's Sons, 1912.

Bosworth, Elsie, *100 Years of Change and Progress, 1872-1972 Fall River Mills Centennial,* Fall River Mills, Fort Crook Historical Society, 1972.

Botta, Paolo Emilio, *Observations on the Inhabitants of California 1827-1828.* Los Angeles, Glen Dawson, 1952.

Bouknight, Marie, and Robert Gruber, Maida Loescher, Richard Meyers, Geraldine Phillips, *Guide to Records in the Military Archives Division Pertaining to Indian-White Relations,* Washington, National Archives and Records Service, 1972.

Bourne, A. Ross, "Some Major Aspects of the Historical Development of Palm Springs Between 1880 and 1938, And in

Addition a Continuation of the Historical Changes in the Indian Land Problem and for Cultural Institutions until 1948," An unpublished M.A. thesis, Occidental College, 1953.

Brown, J. Ross, *The California Indians: A Clever Satire on the Government's Dealings with its Indian Wards.* (A reprint of Cruso's Island.) New York, Harper Brothers, 1864.

Bureau of Indian Affairs, *Estimates of Resident Indian Population and Labor Force Status: By State and Reservation,* Washington, D.C., Government Printing Office, 1973.

California Historical Society, *The Russians in California,* San Francisco, California Historical Society, 1933.

California Indian Rights Association, Inc., *California Indian News,* Los Angeles.

Caughey, J. W., *The Indian of Southern California in 1852: The B. D. Wilson Report and a Selection of Contemporary Comment.* San Marino, California, Huntington Library, 1952.

Cohen, Felix S., *Handbook of Federal Indian Law.* Forword by Harold L. Ikes, Introduction by Nathan R. Margold. Department of the Interior. First Printing, 1941, fourth printing, 1945. Washington, 1945.

Collier, John, *From Every Zenith: A Memoir and Some Essays on Life and Thought,* Denver, Sage Books, 1963.

————, *Indians of the Americas,* New York, Scarborough, Ontario, Mentor Books, 1947.

Conrotto, Eugene L., *Miwok Means People, The Life and Fate of the Native Inhabitants of the California Gold Rush Country.* Fresno, California, Valley Publishers, 1973.

Cook, Sherburne, F., *The Conflict Between the California Indians and White Civilization. Ibero Americana,* nos. 21, 23, 24. Berkeley and Los Angeles, University of California Press, 1943.

————, *The Population of the California Indians, 1769-1970,* Berkeley and Los Angeles, University of California Press, 1976.

202

Cook, Warren L., *Flood Tide of Empire; Spain and the Pacific Northwest 1543-1819,* New Haven and London, Yale University Press, 1973.

Crampton, C. Gregory, ed., *The Mariposa Indian War 1850-1851. Diaries of Robert Eccleston; The California Gold Rush, Yosemite and the High Sierra.* Salt Lake, University of Utah Press, 1957.

Crawford, Richard C., and Charles E. South, *Guide to records in the Civil Archives Division Pertaining to Indian-White Relations,* Washington, National Archives and Record Service, 1972.

Daggett, Stuart, *Chapters in the History of the Southern Pacific,* New York, The Ronald Press, 1922.

Daniels, Roger and Spencer C. Olin, Jr., eds., *Racism in California; A Reader in the History of Oppression.* New York, the Macmillan Company, 1972.

Davies, Carlyle C. and William A. Alderson, *The True Story of Ramona, Its Facts and Fictions, Inspiration and Purpose,* New York.

Davis, W. N., Jr., *Sagebrush Corner: The Opening of California's Northeast.* In the David Agee Horr, *American Indian Ethnohistory* series, New York and London, Garland Publishing, Inc., 1974.

Deloria, Vine, Jr., ed., *Of Utmost Good Faith,* San Francisco, Straight Arrow Books, 1971.

Dennerlein, Gerald Edwin, "The History of Ramonaland: The Economic and Social Development of San Jacinto, California." An unpublished M.A. thesis, University of Southern California, 1940.

Dillon, Richard, *Siskiyou Trail: The Hudson's Bay Company Route to California,* New York, McGraw Hill Book Company, 1975.

Downs, James F., *The Two Worlds of the Wasno. An Indian Tribe of California and Nevada.* New York, Chicago, San Francisco, Toronto, and London, Holt Rinehart and Winston, 1966.

Driver, Harold E., *Excerpts from the Writings of A. L. Kroeber on*

Land Use and Political Organization of California Indians, With Comments by Harold E. Driver. In David Agee Horr, *American Indian Ethnohistory* series, New York and London, Garland, Publishing, Inc., 1974.

DuBois, Constance, *The Condition of the Mission Indians of Southern California*, Philadelphia, Office of the Indian Rights Association, 1901.

Dumke, Glenn S., *The Boom of the Eighties in Southern California*, San Marino, California, Huntington Library, 1944.

Ellis, Richard N., ed., *The Western American Indian. Case Studies in Tribal History*, Lincoln, University of Nebraska Press, 1972.

Ellison, Joseph, *California and the Nation 1850-1869: A Study of the Relations of a Frontier Community with the Federal Government.* Berkeley, University of California Publication in History, Vol. 16, 1927.

Ellison, William Henry, "The United States Indian Policy in California 1846-1860," an unpublished dissertation on file at U.C. Berkeley, 1918.

Engelhardt, Z., *The Missions and Missionaries of California*, San Francisco, James H. Barry Company, 1908-1915.

Fages, Pedro, *A Historical, Political, and Natural Description of California, by Pedro Fages, Soldier of Spain,* translated by Herbert Ingram Priestly, Berkeley, University of California Press, 1937.

Federated Indians of California, *The Smoke Signal of the Federated Indians of California*, Sacramento.

Filler, Louis and Allen Guttman, eds., *The Removal of the Cherokee Nation. Manifest Destiny or National Dishonor?* Lexington, Massachusetts, D. C. Heath and Company, 1962.

Foote, Kate, *The Mission Indians Taxed and Untaxed.* Washington, United States Department of the Interior, Census Office, 11th Census, Government Printing Office, 1890.

Forbes, Jack, *Native Americans of California and Nevada.* Naturegraph Publishers, Healdsburg, California, 1969.

Fort Crook Historical Society, *Reminiscence of Fort Crook Historical Society.* Fall River Mills, California, no date.

Freeman, John F., *A Guide to Manuscripts Relating to the American Indian in the Library of the American Philosophical Society,* Philadelphia, American Philosophical Society, 1966.

Fritz, Henry E., *The Movement for Indian Assimilation 1860-1890,* Philadelphia, University of Pennsylvania, 1963.

Gabbert, John Raymond, *History of Riverside City and County,* Phoenix and Riverside, Record Publishing Company, 1935.

Galbraith, H. Alan, *Equal Justice for California Indians: A Study of the Withdrawal of Federal Services,* An undated manuscript of the 1960's. Berkeley, California Indian Legal Services.

Garcia, Jesse, and Philip Webster, *Location and Character of Indian Lands in California,* Washington, United States Department of Agriculture, 1937.

Gibson, Charles, and Howard Peckham, *Attitudes of the Colonial Powers Toward the American Indians,* Salt Lake City, University of Utah Press, 1969.

Gibson, Charles, *The Aztecs Under Spanish Rule; A History of the Indians of the Valley of Mexico 1519-1810,* Stanford, Stanford University Press, 1964.

—————, *The Black Legend; Anti-Spanish Attitudes in the Old World and the New,* New York, Knopf, 1971.

—————, *Tlaxcala in the Sixteenth Century,* New Haven, Yale University Press, 1952.

Hagan, William Thomas, *Indian Police and Judges; Experiments in Acculturation and Control,* New Haven, Yale University Press, 1966.

Hale, Charles, *Mexican Liberalism in the Age of Mora, 1821-1853,* New Haven, Yale University Press, 1968.

Harvey, Herbert R., *The Luiseno: An Analysis of Change in Patterns of Land Tenure and Social Structure,* in David Agee Horr, *American Indian Ethnohistory* series, New York and London, Garland Publishing, Inc., 1974.

Heizer, Robert F., Haren Nissen and Edward D. Castillo, *California Indian History: A Classified and Annotated Guide to Source Materials,* Ramona, California, Ballena Press, 1975.

Heizer, Robert F., and M. A. Whipple, eds., *The California Indians; A Source Book.* Berkeley, University of California Press, 1951, revised, 1971.

Heizer, Robert F., *Catalogue of the C. Hart Merriam Collection of Data Concerning California Tribes and Other American Indians,* Berkeley, University of California Archaeological Research Facility, Department of Anthropology.

—————, ed., *Census of Non-Reservation California Indians, 1905-1906, by C. E. Kelsey,* Berkeley, University of California Archaeological Research Facility, Department of Anthropology, 1971.

—————, ed., *The Destruction of California Indians.* Santa Barbara and Salt Lake City, Peregrine Smith, Inc., 1974.

—————, *The Four Ages of Tsurai: A Documentary History of the Indian Village of Trinidad Bay,* Los Angeles and Berkeley, University of California Press, 1952.

—————, *The Indians of California: A Critical Bibliography,* Bloomington and London, Indiana University Press, 1976.

—————, *The Indians of Los Angeles County: Hugo Reid's Letters of 1852.* Los Angeles, Southwest Museum, 1968.

—————, *Languages, Territories, and Names of California Indian Tribes,* Berkeley and Los Angeles, University of California Press, 1966.

—————, and Alan F. Almquist, *The Other Californians; Prejudice and Discrimination Under Spain, Mexico, and the United*

States to 1920, Berkeley and Los Angeles, University of California Press, 1971.

—————, *Some Last Century Accounts of the Indians of Southern Californiam* Ramona, California, Bellena Press, 1976.

Henry, Jeannette, ed., *The American Indian Reader,* San Francisco, Indian Historian Press, 1972.

Hill, Edward, *Preliminary Inventory of the Records of the Bureau of Indian Affairs Volume I (Record Group 75),* Washington, National Archives and Records Service, 1965.

—————, *Records in the General Archives Division Relating to American Indians.* Washington, National Archives and Records Services, 1972.

Hill, Joseph J., *The History of Warner's Ranch and its Environs,* Los Angeles, privately printed, 1927.

Hodge, Frederick Webb, ed., *Handbook of the American Indians North of Mexico,* Washington, Smithsonian Institution, Bureau of Ethnology Bulletin 30 (pts. 1 and 2), 1907, 1910.

Hoffman, Ogden, *Reports of Land Cases Determined in the United States District Court for Northern District of California,* San Francisco, 1862.

Holmes, Elmer Wallace, *History of Riverside, California with Biographical Sketches of the Leading Men and Women of the County Who Have Been Identified with its Growth and Development From the Early Days to the Present.* Los Angeles, Historic Record Company, 1912.

Hooper, Lucille, *Coahuilla Indians,* Reprinted with permission of the Regents of the University of California, Ramona, California, Ballena Press, 1972.

Hoopes, A. W., *Indian Affairs and Their Administration with Special Reference to the Far West 1849-1860,* Philadelphia, Oxford University Press, 1932. A Kraus Reprint Co. reprint, 1972.

Horr, David Agee, ed., *American Indian Ethnohistory* series, New York and London, Garland Publishing, Inc., 1974.

Howe, Carrol B., *Ancient Tribes of the Klamath Country,* Portland, Oregon, Binfords and Mort Publishers, 1968.

Hufford, D. A., *The Real Ramona of Helen Hunt Jackson's Famous Novel.* Los Angeles, D. A. Hufford and Company, 1900.

Indian Affairs, Commissioner of, *Reports of the Commissioners of Indian Affairs to the Secretary of the Interior,* Washington, United States Printing Office, published annually.

Indian Claims Commission, *Annual Reports,* Washington, United States Printing Office.

Indian Defense Association of California, *American Indian Life,* San Francisco.

Indian Law Center, University of New Mexico School of Law, *American Indian Law Newsletter.* Albuquerque, New Mexico.

Indian Rights Association, *Indian Truth,* Philadelphia.

Jackson, Helen Hunt, *Ramona,* Boston, Roberts Brothers, San Francisco, 1885.

Jackson, Helen Hunt, *Report on the Condition and Needs of the Mission Indians, 1883.* Reproduced by the San Jacinto Museum, San Jacinto, California.

Jahoda, Gloria, *The Trail of Tears,* New York, Holt Rinehart and Winston, 1975.

James, George Wharton, *In and Out of the Old Missions of California; An Historical and Pictorial Account of the Franciscan Missions,* Boston, Little Brown and Company, 1906.

—————, *Through Ramona's Country,* Boston, Little Brown and Company, 1909.

James, Harry C., *The Coahuilla Indians. The Men Called Master.* Los Angeles, Westernlore Press, 1960.

Johnson, Kenneth M., *K-344 or the California Indians vs. the United States,* Los Angeles, Dawson Book Shop, 1960.

Kelsey, C. E., *Report of the Special Agent For California Indians to the Commissioner of Indian Affairs,* Carlisle, Pennsylvania, Indian School Printing Shop, 1906.

Kenny, Robert W., Attorney General of California, *History of the Proposed Settlement; Claims of California Indians,* Sacramento, State Printing Office, 1944.

Konsag, Ferdinand, *Life and Works of the Reverend Ferdinand Konsag S.J. 1703-1759 an Early Missionary in California by Msgr. M.D.* Krmpotic, Boston, The Stratford Company, 1923.

Kroeber, A. L., *Handbook of the Indians of California,* Washington, Smithsonian Institute, Bureau of American Ethnology, Bulletin 78, 1925.

—————, *Nature of Land-Holding Groups in Aboriginal California.* Berkeley, University of California Archaeological Survey, Report No. 56, 1958, 1962.

Kroeber, Theodora, *Ishi in Two Worlds, A Biography of the Last Wild Indians in North America,* Berkeley and Los Angeles, University of California Press, 1961.

Lawton, Harry, *Willie Boy, A Desert Manhunt,* Balboa Island, California, Paisano Press, 1960.

Lewis, Oscar, *The Big Four: The Story of Huntington, Stanford, Hopkins, and Crocker and the Building of the Central Pacific,* New York, London, A. A. Knopf, 1938.

Lipps, Oscar H., *The Case of the California Indians,* United States Indian Printing Shop, 1932.

Longinos Martinez, Jose, *California in 1792; The Expedition of Jose Longinos Martinez,* San Marino, California, Huntington Library, 1938.

Lounsbury, Ralph G., *Mexican Land Claims in California,* Washington, National Archives and Records Service, 1963.

Malin, J. C., *Indian Policy and Westward Expansion.* Lawrence, Kansas, University of Kansas Press, 1921.

Merriam, C. Hart, *Studies of California Indians.* Berkeley and Los Angeles, University of California Press, 1955.

—————, director, *The Problem of Indian Administration,* Brookings Institution, reprinted with a new introduction by Frank C. Miller, New York and London, Johnson Reprint Corporation, 1971.

Mission Indian Federation, *The Indians: Official Magazine of the Mission Indian Federation.*

Moquin, Wayne, with Charles Van Doren, eds., *A Documentary History of the Mexican Americans,* Toronto and New York, Praeger, 1971.

Moriarity, James Robert, *Chinigehinix: An Indigenous California Indian Religion,* Los Angeles, Southwest Museum, 1969.

Miller, Ronald Dean and Peggy Miller, *The Chemehuevi Indians of Southern California,* Banning, California, Malki Museum Press.

National Archives and Records Service, *Guide to Records in the Civil Archives Division Pertaining to Indian-White Relations,* Washington, National Archives and Records Service, 1972.

—————, *Guide to Records of the Bureau of Indian Affairs in the Archives Branches of the Federal Records Centers,* Washington, National Archives and Records Service, 1972.

—————, *Select Catalog of National Archives Microfilm Publications. The American Indians,* Washington, D.C., National Archives and Records Service, 1972.

—————, *Special Files of the Office of Indian Affairs 1807-1904,* Washington, D.C., National Archives and Records Service, 1971.

Neashman, Ernest R., *Fall River a History,* in the David Agee Horr *American Indian Ethnohistory* series, New York and London, Garland Publishing, Inc., 1974.

Odell, Ruth, *Helen Hunt Jackson (H. H.),* New York and London, D. Appleton-Century Company, Inc., 1939.

Ostrom, Vincent, *Water and Politics: A Study of Water Politics and Administration in the Development of Los Angeles,* Los Angeles, The Haynes Foundation, 1953.

Painter, C. C., *A Visit to the Mission Indians of Southern California and Other Western Tribes,* Philadelphia, Indian Rights Association, 1886.

—————, *A Visit to the Mission Indians of California,* Philadelphia, Indian Rights Association, 1887.

—————, *The Condition of Affairs in Indian Territories and California. A Report by Professor C. C. Painter, Agent of the Indian Rights Association,* Philadelphia, Indian Rights Association, 1888.

Parker, Horace, *The Treaty of Temecula,* Balboa Island, California, Paisano Press, 1967.

Parry, J. H., *The Spanish Seaborn Empire,* New York, Alfred A. Knopf, 1966.

Payne, Doris P., *Captain Jack, Modoc Renegade,* Portland, Oregon, Binford and Mort, 1938.

Pearce, Roy H., *The Savages of America: A Study of the Indian and the Idea of Civilization.* Baltimore, Johns Hopkins Press, 1953.

—————, *Savagism and Civilization: A Study of the Indian and the American Mind,* Baltimore, Johns Hopkins Press, 1967.

Peckham, Howard and Charles Gibson, eds., *Attitudes of Colonial Powers Towards the American Indian,* Salt Lake City, University of Utah Press, 1969.

Phillips, George Harwood, *Chiefs and Challengers: Indian Resistance and Cooperation in Southern California,* Berkeley and Los Angeles, University of California Press, 1975.

Pletcher, David M., *Diplomacy of Annexation: Texas, Oregon, and the Mexican War,* Columbia, Missouri, University of Missouri Press, 1974.

Powell, Philip Wayne, *Soldiers, Indians, and Silver; North Ameri-*

ca's First Frontier War, Berkeley and Los Angeles, University of California Press, 1971.

Powers, S., *Tribes of California,* Contribution to North American Ethnology, Department of the Interior, United States Geographical and Geological Survey of the Rocky Mountain Region, vol. 3, Washington, United States Printing Office, 1877.

Price, Monroe E., *Law and the American Indian: Readings, Notes, and Cases,* New York, Bobbs Merrill Company, 1973.

— — — — —, *Native American Law Manual,* Los Angeles, California Indian Legal Service, 1970.

Prucha, Francis Paul, ed., *Documents of United States Indian Policy,* Lincoln, University of Nebraska Press, 1975.

— — — — —, *The Indians in American History,* New York, Chicago, San Francisco, Atlanta, Dallas, Montreal, Toronto, Sydney, Holt, Rinehart and Winston, 1971.

Quimby, Garfield M., *History of the Potrero Ranch and its Neighbors,* San Bernardino, Quarterly of the San Bernardino County Museum Association, vol. 22, no. 2, winter, 1975.

Riddell, F. A., comp., *A Bibliography of the Indians of Southern California,* Sacramento, State of California Resource Agency, Department of Parks and Recreation Division of Beaches and Parks, 1962.

Riddle, Jeff C., *The Indian History of the Modoc War,* Eugene, Oregon, Union Press, 1974.

Robinson, William W., *The Indians of Los Angeles; Story of the Liquidation of a People,* Los Angeles, Dawson Books, 1952.

Rockwell, John, *The Status of the Indians in California Today,* Sacramento, Sacramento Indian Agency, 1944.

Ross, Norman A., *Index to the Decisions of the Indian Claims Commission,* New York, Clearwater Press, 1973.

— — — — —, *Index to the Expert Testimony Before the Indian Claims Commission,* New York, Clearwater Press, 1973.

Royce, C. C., comp., *Indian Land Cessions in the United States,* Washington, Bureau of American Ethnology Annual Report 18, 1899.

Sales, Father Luis O. P., *Observations on California 1772-1790.* Translated and edited by Charles Rudkin, Los Angeles, Dawson Books, 1956.

Sanchez, Nellie Van de Grift, *Spanish Arcadia,* Los Angeles, Powell Publishing, 1929.

San Martin, Jose, *Memorial and Proposals of Senor Don Jose San Martin of the Californias,* San Francisco, Grabhorn Press, 1945.

Saunders, Charles Francis and J. Smeaton Chase, *The California Padres and the Missions,* Boston and New York, Houghton Mifflin Company, 1915.

Seymour, Charles Francis, "Relations Between the United States Government and the Mission Indians of Southern California," an unpublished M.A. thesis, University of California, Berkeley, 1906.

Spencer, Robert F. and Jesse D. Jennings, eds., *The Native Americans,* New York, Harper and Row, 1965.

Spicer, Edward H., *Cycles of Conquest: The Impact of Spain, Mexico, and the United States on the Indians of the Southwest, 1533-1960,* Tucson, University of Arizona Press, 1962.

Steiner, Stanley, *The New Indians,* New York, Evanston, and London, Harper and Row Publishers, 1968.

Stevens, Robert J., *Report of Colonel Robert J. Stevens, Special Commissioner to Make an Investigation and Report upon Indian Affairs in California,* Washington, Government Publications Office, 1868.

Strong, William Duncan, *Aboriginal Society in Southern California.* Reprint from University of California Publication in American Archaeology and Ethnology, vol. 26, 1926, Banning, California, Malki Museum Press, 1972.

Sutton, Imre, *Indian Land Tenure: Bibliographical Essays and a Guide to the Literature,* New York, Clearwater Publishing Co., 1975.

—————, "Land, Tenure, and Changing Occupations on Indian Reservations in Southern California," a dissertation in geography, University of California, Los Angeles, 1964.

Tapper, Violet and Nellie Lolmaugh, *The Friendly Valley,* Hemet, California, privately printed.

The American Association on Indian Affairs, Inc., *Indian Affairs,* New York.

Thomas, Richard M., "The Mission Indians: A Case Study in Leadership and Cultural Change," a dissertation, University of California, Los Angeles, 1964.

Trennert, Robert A., Jr., *Alternatives to Extinction: Federal Indian Policy and the Beginnings of the Reservation System 1846-51,* Philadelphia, Temple University Press, 1975.

Underhill, Ruth, *Indians of Southern California,* Lawrence, Kansas, Department of the Interior, Bureau of Indian Affairs, 1941.

United States Code, Title 25, *Indians.*

United States Congress, House, *Hearings,* 1848-.

United States Congress, House, *Reports,* 1848-.

United States Congress, Senate, *Hearings,* 1848-.

United States Congress, Senate, *Reports,* 1848-.

University of Oklahoma College of Law, *American Indian Law Review,* Norman, Oklahoma.

Vandever, William, *Mission Indians of California. Report of William Vandever, United States Indian Inspector,* Washington, Government Printing Office, 1876.

Vedeer, William H., *Federal Encroachment on Indian Water Rights and the Impairment of Reservation Development.*

Warren, Charles, *The Supreme Court in United States History,* 2 vols., Boston, Little Brown, and Company, 1926.

Washburn, Wilcomb E., *Red Man's Land/White Man's Law: A Study of the Past and Present Status of the American Indian.* New York, Charles Scribner's Sons, 1971.

Webb, E. B., *Indian Life at the Old Missions,* Los Angeles, W. F. Lewis, 1952.

Wetmore, Charles, *Report of Charles A. Wetmore. Special U.S. Commissioner, Mission Indians of Southern California,* Washington, Government Printing Office, 1875.

Wheeler, Lt. George M., *Annual Report upon the Geographical Surveys West of the One Hundredth Meridian in California, Nevada, Utah, Wyoming, New Mexico, Arizona, Montana,* Washington, Government Printing Office, 1876.

Wheeler-Voegelin, Erminie, *Pit River Indians of California: Fall River Valley. An Examination of Historical Sources,* in the David Agee Horr *American Indian Ethnohistory* series, New York and London, Garland Publishing, Inc., 1974.

White, R. C., *Luiseno Social Organization,* Berkeley, University of California Publications in American Archaeology and Ethnology, vol. 48, no. 2, pp. 19-194, 1946.

Willis, Purl, ed., *The Indian* (a journal), San Diego.

Wilson, B. D., *The Indians of Southern California in 1852,* J. W. Caughey ed., San Marino, California, Huntington Library, 1952.

Windeer, William A., *Lieut. William A. Windeer's Report April 29, 1856, on a Visit to Chief Antonio at Rancho San Jacinto,* 34th Congress, 3rd session, House Exec. Doc. 76, Washington, Government Printing Office, 1856.

Wolcott, Marjorie T., ed., *Pioneer Notes from the Diaries of Judge Benjamin Hayes 1849-75,* Los Angeles, Privately printed, 1929.

Wolf, Eric, *Sons of the Shaking Earth,* Chicago and London, University of Chicago Press, 1959.

Wollenberg, Charles, ed., *Ethnic Conflict in California History*, Los Angeles, Tinnon-Brown, Inc., Book Publishers, 1970.

Young, James R., Dennis Moristo, G. David Tenebaum, *An Inventory of the Mission Indian Records*, Los Angeles, University of California, Los Angeles, American Indian Studies Center, 1976.

—————, *An Inventory of the Pala Indian Agency Records*, Los Angeles, University of California, Los Angeles, American Indian Studies Center, 1976.

ARTICLES

Alcorn, Greg, "Racial Attitudes Justifying Indian Removal 1820-1832," Unpublished.

Anonymous, "Occupancy Rights of Indians in Mexican Cession Area, What Constitutes Extinguishment of Occupancy Rights," *George Washington Law Review*, 10 (April, 1942), 753-755.

Anonymous, "Systematic Discrimination in the Indian Claims Commission: The Burden of Proof in Redressing Historical Wrongs," *Iowa Law Review*, 57 (June, 1972), 1300-1319.

Brown, J. Ross, "The Coast Rangers, II, The Indian Reservations," *Harpers Magazine*, 23 (1861), 306–316.

Burke, Joseph C., "The Cherokee Cases: A Study in Law, Politics, and Morality," *Stanford Law Review*, 21 (February, 1969).

Carter, Nancy Carol, "Race and Power Politics as Aspects of Federal Guardianship over American Indians: Land-Related Cases, 1887-1924," *American Indian Law Review*, 4 (Winter, 1976), 197-248.

Cohen, Felix S., "Original Indian Title," *Minnesota Law Review*, 32 (December, 1942), 28-59.

—————, "The Spanish Origin of Indian Rights in the Law of the United States," *Georgetown Law Journal,* 31 (1942), 1–21.

Cook, S. F., "The California Indian and Anglo American Culture," in Charles Wollenberg, *Ethnic Conflict in California History,* Los Angeles, Tinnon-Brown, Inc., 1970.

—————, "The Destruction of the California Indians," *California Monthly,* 74 (December, 1968), 15-19.

—————, "The Epidemics of 1830-1833 in California and Oregon," *University of California Publication in American Archaeology and Ethnology,* 43, pt. 3 (1955), 303-326.

—————, "The Mechanisms and Extent of Dietary Adaptation Among Certain Groups of California and Nevada Indians," *Ibero-Americana,* 18 (1941).

—————, "Population Trends Among the California Mission Indians," *Ibero-Americana,* 17 (1940).

Coy, P. E. B., "Justice for the Indians in Eighteenth Century Mexico," *American Journal of Legal History,* 14 (January, 1968), 41-49.

Croughter, Richard E., and Andrew F. Rolle, "Edward Fitzgerald Beale and the Indian Peace Commissioners in California," *Historical Society of California Quarterly,* 42 (June, 1960).

Cutter, Donald C., "Clio and the California Indian Claims," *The Journal of the West,* 14 (October, 1975), 35-48.

Davidson, David M., "Negro Slave Control and Resistance in Colonial Mexico 1519-1650," *Hispanic American Historical Review,* 46 (August, 1966), 235-253.

Davis, Carlyle C., "Ramona: The Ideal and the Real," *Out West,* 19 (December, 1904), 575-596.

Ellison, W. H., "The Federal Indian Policy in California, 1846-1860," *Mississippi Valley Historical Review,* 9 (1922), 37-67.

Garner, Van Hastings, "The Treaty of Guadalupe Hidalgo and

the California Indians: Where are the Historians?", *The Indian Historian,* 9 (Winter, 1976), 10-13.

Gates, P. W., "Ajudication of Spanish-Mexican Land Claims in California," *Huntington Library Quarterly,* 21 (1958).

Geary, G. J., "Secularization of the California Indian Missions," *Studies in American Church History,* 17 (1934).

Gibson, A. M., "Sources for Research on the American Indian," *Ethnohistory,* 7 (1960), 121-136.

Goodrich, Chancey Shafter, "The Legal Status of the California Indians," *California Law Review,* 14 (1926), 1-48, 83-100, 157-187.

Grossman, George, Rennard Strictland, Hans Walker, Victoria S. Santana, Larry Leveanthal, "Sources of American Indian Law," *Law Library Journal,* 6 (November, 1974), 465-466.

Harvard Law Review, "United States Must Compensate for Appropriation of Lands Occupied by Tribes under Original Indian Title," *Harvard Law Review,* 60 (February, 1947), 465-466.

Heizer, Robert E., "Alexander S. Taylor's Map of Indian Tribes, 1864," *California Historical Society Quarterly,* 20 (June, 1941), 171-180.

Henderson, J. Youngblood, "Unraveling the Riddle of Aboriginal Title," *American Indian Law Review,* 5 (Summer, 1977), 75-137.

Hutchinson, C. Alan, "The Mexican Government and the Mission Indians of Upper California, 1821-1835," *The Americas,* 21 (April, 1965), 334-362.

Hurtado, Albert, "Controlling Native Californians: California Indian Relations During the Mexican War," unpublished.

Kelly, Lawrence C., "The Indian Reorganization Act: The Dream and the Reality," *Pacific Historical Review,* 44 (August, 1975), 291-312.

Kennedy, Robert F., "Buying it Back from the Indians," *Life,* 52, no. 2 (March 23, 1962), 17-19.

Lewis, F. D., "The Warner's Ranch Indians and Why They Were Removed to Pala," *Overland Monthly,* 42 (1903), 171-173.

Lummis, Charles F., "The Sequoya League," *Out West,* 16 (June 1902), 407-413.

Mather, Mary E. Fleming, "The Case for Using Historical Data: Third Generation Tribal Nationalism," *The Indian Historian,* 6 (Fall, 1973), 14-19.

Mawn, Geoffrey P., "A Land-Grant Guarantee: The Treaty of Guadalupe Hidalgo or the Protocol of Queretaro?", *Journal of the West,* 14 (October, 1975), 49-63.

Merriam, C. Hart, "The Indian Population of California," *The American Anthropologist,* n.s. 7 (1905), 594-606.

Reynolds, Osborne M., "Agua Caliente Revisited: Recent Developments as to Zoning of Indian Reservations," *American Indian Law Review,* 4 (Winter, 1976), 249-267.

Rogers, Carl Bryant, "Zoning: A Rebuttal to 'Village of Euclid Meets Agua Caliente,'" *American Indian Law Review,* 4 (Summer, 1976), 141-168.

Servin, Manuel P., "The Secularization of the California Missions: A Reappraisal," *Southern California Quarterly,* 47, (1965), 133-149.

Stewart, O. C., "Kroeber and the Indian Claims Commission Case," *Kroeber Anthropological Society Papers,* 25, (1961), 181-190.

Taylor, William B., "Land and Water Rights in the Viceroyalty of New Spain," *New Mexico Historical Review,* 50, (July, 1975).

Veeder, William H., "Water Rights: Life and Death for the American Indian," *The Indian Historian,* 5 (Summer, 1972), 4-21.

White, R. C., "The Luiseno Theory of Knowledge," *American Anthropologist,* 59 (1957), 1-19.

Williamson, Mrs. M. Burton, "Soboba Indians of Southern California," *Out West,* 30 (January-June, 1909), 148-158.

Young, Ronald T. L., "Interagency Conflicts of Interest: The Peril to Indian Water Rights," *Law and Social Order,* (1972), 313-328.

NEWSPAPERS

Hemet News, Hemet, California

Intermountain News, Burney, California

Los Angeles Examiner, Los Angeles, California

Los Angeles Express, Los Angeles, California

Los Angeles Times, Los Angeles, California

Palm Springs Desert Sun, Palm Springs, California

Palm Springs Limelight, Palm Springs, California

Palm Springs News, Palm Springs, California

Riverside Enterprise, Riverside, California

Riverside Press Enterprise, Riverside, California

Riverside Press, Riverside, California

Sacramento Bee, Sacramento, California

San Diego Tribune, San Diego, California

San Francisco Chronicle, San Francisco, California

San Jacinto Register, San Jacinto, California

Warpath, San Francisco, California

Wassaja, San Francisco, California

ARCHIVAL SOURCES

National Archives, Washington, D.C.

Record Group 75, Bureau of Indian Affairs
    Letters Received 1824-1881
    Letters Sent 1824-1881

Record Group 48, Records of the Indian Division, Office of the Secretary of the Interior
  Letters Sent 1849-1903

Record Group 94, Records of the Adjutant General's Office, 1780-1917
  Letters Received by the Office of the Adjutant General (main series) 1822-1860
  Letters Received by the Office of the Adjutant General (main series) 1871-1880
  Letters Received by the Office of the Adjutant General 1881-1889
  Letters Sent by the Governors and Secretaries of the State of California 1847-1920

Record Group 393, Records of the United States Army Continental Commands 1821-1920
  Records of the 10th Military Department 1846-1851
  Records of the Department of the Columbia 1865-1913
  Records of the Department (and Division) of the Pacific 1848-1866
  Records of the District of the Lakes 1868-1873
  Records of the District of Southern California 1861–1866
  Records of the District of California 1864–1866
  Letters Sent from Camp Wright 1862-1869
  Letters Sent and Received between 1864 and 1866 by Fort Gaston. Letters Received 1879-1886

National Archives
Federal Archives and Records Center, San Bruno
Papers of Col. Lafayette A. Dorrington, Special Agent, Bureau of Indian Affairs, 1913-1930
Records of various northern California agencies listed under Digger, Ft. Bidwell, Greenville, Hoopa, Roseburg, Round Valley, Tule River, and Sacramento Area Office.

National Archives,
Federal Archives and Record Center, Laguna Nigel
Mission Indian Agency Records

Records of the Pala Subagency
Records of the Riverside Area Field Office
Records of the Palm Springs Agency

University of California, Berkeley (Bancroft Library)
C. Hart Merriam Collection
Papers of the California League for American Indians

University of California, Los Angeles
Papers of the American Indian Defense Association

University of California, Santa Barbara
The Pearl Chase Collection

Papers of the Indian Rights Association, Philadelphia

Index

225